Contents

Introduction

The National Council of Teachers of Mathematics (NCTM) has set specific standards to help students become confident of their mathematical abilities. Communicating mathematically and problem solving are the keys to helping students develop skills to apply in their daily lives and in later careers.

Based on the belief that students learn to reason mathematically in order to become problem-solvers, the strategies in this book show students more than one way to solve problems. These strategies are not absolute techniques, however. Learning a multitude of ways to approach a problem is part of the philosophy in developing sets of problem-solving strategies.

Organization

The chapters offer several strategies to solve a given type of problem: Graphs, Logic, Addition and Subtraction, Multiplication, Division, Fractions, Fractions and Mixed Numbers, Measurement, Decimals and Fractions, and Metrics.

Special Feature

Each chapter concludes with a "Flex Your Math Muscles" activity page that presents an opportunity for students to choose their own strategy to solve problems. These pages provide students with a unique way to approach the challenges. Divergent thinking is promoted in these lessons.

Problem Solving Strategies

The following problem solving strategies are demonstrated:

CHOOSE AN OPERATION   Students determine which operation (addition, subtraction, multiplication, or division) to use based on the information presented.

USE ESTIMATION   Students learn both when and how to estimate answers, based on rounding numbers and performing the appropriate operation. Estimation is encouraged as a strategy in all problem solving to verify reasonableness of answers.

FIND A PATTERN   This strategy emphasizes pattern recognition of given sequences of numbers, geometric shapes, pictorial information, and other data for problem solving.

GUESS AND CHECK   Students learn a variety of methods to reduce the number of trial and error efforts needed to reach accuracy in answers.

IDENTIFY EXTRA OR MISSING INFORMATION   By identifying pertinent information, students learn to recognize information that is extra or missing.

MAKE/USE A DRAWING   Creating visual images of information makes analysis of the facts easier.

MAKE A CHART   Students learn to organize information into meaningful lists for later matching or computation.

MAKE A TABLE   Pattern recognition, identification of extra or missing information, and arrangement of data into a visual form demonstrate the effectiveness of making a table.

USE A GRAPH   Graphing organizes information so that comparisons can be made visually.

IDENTIFY SUBSTEPS   Some complex problems require the completion of more than one step to calculate the solution. This strategy emphasizes the importance of identifying both the given information and the order of operations to reach the solution.

USE LOGICAL REASONING   In this strategy students learn to recognize relationships and to answer the question, "Does it make sense?" Strategies include a process of elimination of answers and visual representation of information to organize the elements of a problem.

WORK BACKWARD   This section introduces a strategy for solving complex problems in which the end result is given. By recognizing clue words and using them to solve the problem, students can work backward from an answer. This skill develops background for later success in algebra.

WRITE A NUMBER SENTENCE   Converting written statements into numerical sentences to solve for an unknown is the basis of an algebraic approach. This strategy demonstrates identification of known and unknown information to develop sentences for solutions.

USE A FORMULA   Learning to use formulas to solve for unknowns develops a foundation for success in algebra.

Use

This book is designed for independent use by students who have had instruction in the specific skills covered in these lessons. Copies of the activities can be given to individuals, pairs of students, or small groups for completion. They can also be used as a center activity. If students are familiar with the content, the worksheets can be homework for reviewing and reinforcing problem-solving concepts.

To begin, determine the implementation that fits your students' needs and your classroom structure. The following plan suggests a format for this implementation:

1. *Explain* the purpose of the worksheets to your class.
2. *Review* the mechanics of how you want students to work with the exercises.
3. *Review* the specific skill for the students who may not remember the process for successful completion of the computation.
4. *Introduce* students to the process and to the purpose of the activities.
5. *Do* a practice activity together.
6. *Allow* students to experiment, discover, and explore a variety of ways to solve a given problem.

Additional Notes

1. *Bulletin Board.* Display completed worksheets to show student progress.
2. *Center Activities.* Use the worksheets as center activities to give students the opportunity to work cooperatively.

3. *Have fun.* Working with these activities can be fun as well as meaningful for you and your students.

What Research Says

The National Council of Teachers of Mathematics (NCTM) has listed problem solving as a key standard for instructional programs for all students. According to NCTM,

> Problem solving is the cornerstone of school mathematics. Without the ability to solve problems, the usefulness and power of mathematical ideas, knowledge, and skills are severely limited. Students who can efficiently and accurately multiply but who cannot identify situations that call for multiplication are not well prepared. Students who can both develop *and* carry out a plan to solve a mathematical problem are exhibiting knowledge that is much deeper and more useful than simply carrying out a computation. Unless students can solve problems, the facts, concepts, and procedures they know are of little use. The goal of school mathematics should be for all students to become increasingly able and willing to engage with and solve problems.
>
> Problem solving is also important because it can serve as a vehicle for learning new mathematical ideas and skills (Schroeder and Lester 1989). A problem-centered approach to teaching mathematics uses interesting and well-selected problems to launch mathematical lessons and engage students. In this way, new ideas, techniques, and mathematical relationships emerge and become the focus of discussion. Good problems can inspire the exploration of important mathematical ideas, nurture persistence, and reinforce the need to understand and use various strategies, mathematical properties, and relationships.

National Council of Teachers of Mathematics. *Principles and Standards for School Mathematics.* Reston, Va.: The National Council of Teachers of Mathematics, 2000.

Schroeder, Thomas L., and Frank K. Lester, Jr. "Developing Understanding in Mathematics via Problem Solving." In *New Directions for Elementary School Mathematics,* 1989 Yearbook of the National Council of Teachers of Mathematics, edited by Paul R. Trafton, pp. 31–42. Reston, Va.: National Council of Teachers of Mathematics, 1989.

Correlation to NCTM Standards

Content Strands	Pages
Number and Operations	
Understand the place-value structure of the base-ten number system and be able to represent and compare whole numbers and decimals	89, 90, 91, 92
Understand the effects of multiplying and dividing	39, 40, 41, 46, 47, 48, 49, 50, 52, 53, 54, 55, 56, 57, 58
Develop fluency with basic number combinations for multiplication and division and use these combinations to mentally compute problems	39, 40, 41, 46, 47, 48, 49, 50, 52, 53, 54, 55, 56, 57, 58, 108
Develop fluency in adding, subtracting, multiplying, and dividing	33, 34, 35, 36, 37, 38, 39, 40, 41, 46, 47, 48, 49, 50, 52, 53, 54, 55, 56, 57, 58, 105, 106, 107, 108
Develop and use strategies to estimate computations involving decimals in situations relevant to students' experience	48, 50, 55, 89, 90, 91, 92, 95, 96, 97, 98, 105, 106, 107
Use visual models, benchmarks, and equivalent forms to add and subtract decimals	93, 94, 95, 96, 97, 98
Develop understanding of fractions as parts of unit wholes	59, 60, 68
Recognize and generate equivalent forms of commonly used fractions	59, 60, 62, 69, 70, 71, 72
Use models, benchmarks, and equivalent forms to judge the size of fractions	59, 60, 63, 65
Describe classes of numbers according to characteristics such as the nature of their factors	18, 70, 71, 72
Develop and use strategies to estimate computations involving fractions	61, 69
Use visual models, benchmarks, and equivalent forms to add and subtract commonly used fractions	61, 62, 63, 64, 65, 66, 67, 68, 69, 70, 71, 72, 73, 74, 75, 76, 77, 78

Problem Solving Strategies 5, SV 0516-2

Content Strands	Pages
Algebra	
Describe, extend, and make generalizations about numeric patterns	91
Geometry	
Identify, compare, and analyze attributes of two- and three-dimensional shapes and develop vocabulary to describe the attributes	79, 85
Measurement	
Understand such attributes as length and area, and select the appropriate type of unit for measuring each attribute	79, 85, 86, 87, 88
Develop, understand, and use formulas to find the area of rectangles and related triangles and parallelograms	79
Understand the need for measuring with standard units and become familiar with standard units in the customary and metric systems	80, 81, 82, 83, 84, 99, 100, 101, 102, 104, 105
Carry out simple unit conversions, such as from centimeters to meters, within a system of measurement	80, 81, 82, 83, 84, 99, 100, 101, 103, 104
Select and use benchmarks to estimate measurements	80, 81, 82, 83, 84
Data Analysis and Probability	
Collect data using observations, surveys, and experiments	16, 17, 18, 19, 20, 21, 22, 23, 24, 25, 26, 27, 28, 29, 30, 31
Represent data using tables and graphs such as line plots, bar graphs, and line graphs	9, 10, 11, 12, 13, 14, 15, 16, 17, 18, 19, 20, 21, 22, 23, 24, 25, 54, 55, 105, 106, 107, 108
Propose and justify conclusions and predictions that are based on data and design studies to further investigate the conclusions or predictions	9, 10, 11, 12, 13, 14, 16, 17, 18, 22, 23, 24, 25, 26, 27, 28, 29, 30, 31, 54, 55
Problem Solving	
Build new mathematical knowledge through problem solving	all
Solve problems that arise in mathematics and in other contexts	all
Apply and adapt a variety of appropriate strategies to solve problems	all
Monitor and reflect on the process of mathematical problem solving	all

Problem Solving Strategies 5, SV 0516-2

Name _____ Date _____

ASSESSMENT, page 1
....

Follow the directions to solve each problem.

Identify which type of graph would best represent the set of information. Use *bar*, *line*, or *pie*.

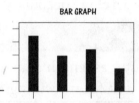 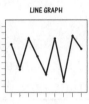

BAR GRAPH   LINE GRAPH   PIE GRAPH

   1. Daily average
   temperature for a month: _____

Underline what you need. Cross out what you do not need. Solve the problem.

   2. Your mother goes to the store. She has $25. She gives
   the clerk a $20 bill. He gives her $9.50 change.
   How much did your mother spend?   _____

Work backward. Then solve the problem.

   3. Carlos trades 12 comic books for 8 of Jan's. He trades 5 for
   6 of Pete's. He has 20 books now. How many did he begin with?

   _____

Determine what operations you need. Solve the problem.

   4. Philip trades 3 sets of football cards for 5 sets of hockey cards. There are
   10 cards in each set of football cards. There are 8 cards in each set of hockey
   cards. How many more cards did Philip have after the trade?

   _____

Guess and check to solve the problems.

   5. Jorge is 1 year older than Julia. The product of their ages is 240.

   How old is each? _____   _____

Choose the correct operation and solve the problem.

   6. Katrina sets 12 plates around the table for her guests. If she places 6 tiny
   prizes on each plate, how many prizes will she need in all?

   _____

6

ASSESSMENT, page 2

Round the numbers. Then estimate to solve the problem.

7. To earn her pilot's license, Kahva must fly 19,927 miles. She plans 38 flights. About how many miles must she fly on each flight?

_____

Use the drawing to write a fraction for the shaded parts.

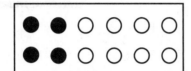

8. _____

Find the least common multiples of the denominators. Then solve the problem.

9. Sherry had $2\frac{1}{2}$ apple pies. She gave away $\frac{1}{3}$ of one of the pies.

How much did she have left? _____

Use logic and a table to solve the problem.

10. Yvonne, Jerry, and Elena finished first, second, and third in the spelling bee. Jerry was not first. Elena finished between the other two. Who finished first, who finished second, and who finished third?

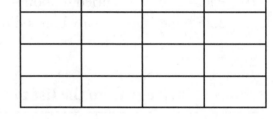

1st _____ 2nd _____ 3rd _____

Use the formula to solve the problem.
Copy the formula and use the numbers in the formula. $A = s \times s$

11. Mrs. George wants a square rug for the living room. One side is 5 feet. How much area will it cover?

_____

ASSESSMENT, page 3

**Estimate the capacity and identify the appropriate unit.
Use *cup*, *pint*, *quart*, or *gallon*.**

12. a swimming pool _____

**To change the unit of measure, use the chart.
Choose an operation. Solve the problem.**

| 1 pound (lb) = 16 ounces (oz) |
| 1 ton (T) = 2,000 pounds |

13. The concrete used for a driveway weighs
10,000 pounds.

How many tons is this? _____

Find and write the pattern. Then solve the problem.

14. What are the missing numbers in this pattern?

64.0   58.5   53   47.5   _____   _____   31.0   25.5   _____

**Look for clues. Change all fractions or all decimals.
Write a number sentence. Solve the problem.**

15. Paul's two dogs buried $4\frac{1}{2}$ bones. One dog buried
2.25 bones. How many bones did the other dog bury?

_____

Choose a strategy from the list to solve the problem.

Choose an Operation	Make a Drawing	Use Guess and Check	Identify Substeps
Use a Chart	Use Logic	Use Estimation	Work Backward

16. You have $51 to spend on shirts. They cost $11.25 each.
Can you buy 5 shirts?

Strategy _____   Answer _____

Name _____ Date _____

DON'T LAUGH AT A GRAPH

Strategy: Use a Graph

Graphs are pictures of information. They make information easier to compare. There are 3 kinds of graphs: bar graphs, line graphs, and pie graphs. Bar graphs and line graphs can be vertical or horizontal. A vertical bar graph is shown at the right.

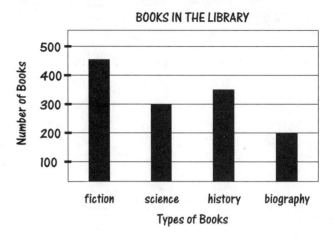

(STEP 1) Read the title of the graph.
The title tells you what the graph is about.

(STEP 2) Read the bottom of the graph.
Put your finger on the name of a type of book at the bottom of the graph. Move your finger to the top of the bar that stands for that type.

(STEP 3) Read the scale on the graph.
Move your finger left to the scale. The number there tells you the number of that type of book.

Try It! Use the information on the graph to solve these problems.

1. Which type has the greatest number of books in the library?

   _____

2. Which type has the least number of books in the library?

   _____

3. Are there more books of fiction or books of biography?

   _____

4. How does the graph make it easier to tell whether there are more fiction books or more biographies?

   _____

5. About how many more books of fiction are there than biographies?

   _____

6. About what is the total number of books in the library?

   _____

Name _____ Date _____

LAZY BAR GRAPH

Strategy: Use a Graph

Bar graphs can be either vertical or horizontal. In either case, the heights or lengths of the bars make it easy to compare data. A horizontal bar graph is shown at the right.

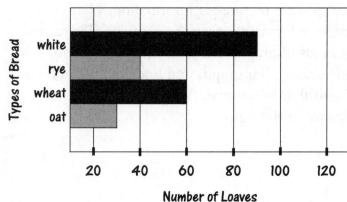

STEP 1 **Read the title of the graph.**
This graph is about bread.

STEP 2 **Read the side of the graph.**
Put your finger on the name of a type on the vertical line at the left side. In this case, the groups are kinds of bread. Move your finger right to the end of the bar for that group.

STEP 3 **Read the scale on the graph.**
Move down to the scale at the bottom of the graph. The number there tells you the number of loaves of that kind of bread.

Try It! Use the information on the graph to solve these problems.

1. Which kind of bread do they bake the greatest number of loaves?

_____

2. Which kind do they bake the least number of loaves?

_____

3. Do they bake more white bread or more rye bread?

_____

4. Do they bake more wheat bread or more rye bread?

_____

5. About how many more loaves of white bread than wheat bread do they bake?

_____

6. About what is the total number of loaves of bread baked?

_____

Name _____   Date _____

BAR GRAPHS SIDE BY SIDE

Strategy: Use a Graph

Bar graphs are used to compare information. You can even look at two separate bar graphs to compare information. But sometimes it is easier if the two bar graphs are joined into one double-bar graph.

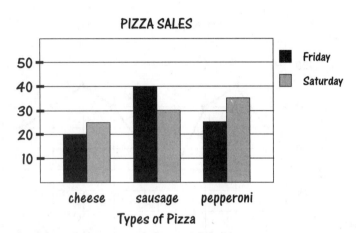

STEP 1 **Read the title of the graph.**
This graph is about pizza sales.

STEP 2 **Read the key.**
Friday sales are shown in black bars, and Saturday sales are shown in gray bars.

STEP 3 **Compare the bars.**
Look at the graph to see how the bars are different for the two days. Move your finger to the top of the bar for Friday. Then move it to the top of the bar for Saturday. The higher bar represents the greater number.

Try It!   Use the information on the graph to solve these problems.

1. On what day were there more cheese pizzas sold?

_____

2. On what day were there fewer sausage pizzas sold?

_____

3. How many more pepperoni pizzas were sold on Saturday than on Friday?

_____

4. Which pizza appears to be the most popular? How does the graph support your answer?

_____

_____

Name _____ Date _____

LINE UP WITH LINE GRAPHS

Strategy: Use a Graph

Line graphs are often used to show how data changes over time. This graph shows the school attendance rate by month.

STEP 1 **Read the title.**

STEP 2 **Read the bottom of the graph.**
Put your finger on a month on the bottom of the graph. Move your finger up to the dot for that month.

STEP 3 **Read the scale.**
Move your finger to the left to find the percentage rate.

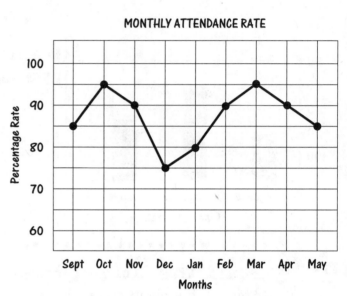

MONTHLY ATTENDANCE RATE

Percentage Rate

Months: Sept Oct Nov Dec Jan Feb Mar Apr May

Try It! Use the information on the graph to solve the problems.

1. How much greater was attendance in September than in December?

   _____

2. In which 2 months was the attendance rate the highest?

   _____ _____

3. Attendance was how much greater in the highest month than in the lowest month?

   _____

4. In what 3 months was the attendance rate the same?

   _____ _____ _____

5. In which month did the attendance rate fall the greatest amount?

   _____

6. Was the attendance rate higher in September–December or February–May?

   _____

Name _____ Date _____

LINE GRAPHS DON'T LIE

Strategy: Use a Graph

Double line graphs are often used to compare monthly information for different years. This double line graph compares the monthly attendance for 2 years.

STEP 1 ▷ **Read the title.**

STEP 2 ▷ **Read the key.**
Read the solid line for 2005 data. Read the dashed line for 2006 data.

STEP 3 ▷ **Compare the lines.**

─────── 2005   ─ ─ ─ ─ 2006

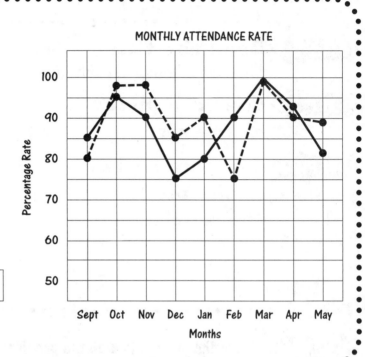

MONTHLY ATTENDANCE RATE

Try It!   Use the information on the graph to solve the problems.

1. In which year was the overall attendance rate higher?

_____

2. In which 2 months and year did the attendance rate remain the same?

_____   _____

3. In which months was the 2006 rate lower than the 2005 rate?

_____   _____   _____

4. In which month and year was the attendance rate the lowest?

_____   _____

5. In which month was the attendance rate the same for both years?

_____

6. Which month had the greatest difference in the attendance rate between 2005 and 2006?

_____

Problem Solving Strategies 5, SV 0516-2

Name _____ Date _____

NOT LIKE MOM'S APPLE PIE

Strategy: Use a Graph

A pie graph looks just like it sounds, a pie. Each slice of the pie is a piece of information included in the whole pie. The size of each piece shows its relationship to the whole and to each other piece of the pie.

STEP 1 **Read the title.**
This graph shows a monthly budget.

STEP 2 **Compare pieces of the pie.**

STEP 3 **Compare a piece of the pie to the whole.**

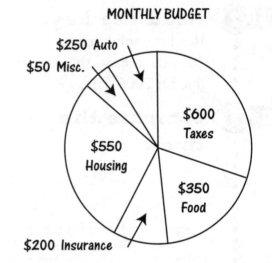

MONTHLY BUDGET

$250 Auto
$50 Misc.
$600 Taxes
$550 Housing
$350 Food
$200 Insurance

Try It! Use the information on the graph to solve the problems.

1. Which expense is the largest part of this budget?

   _____

2. Which expenses are similar in amount?

   _____

3. What is the total budget in this graph?

   _____

4. What is the difference between the greatest expense and the least expense?

   _____

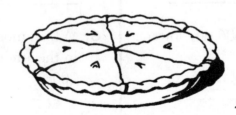

Name _____ Date _____

BAR, LINE, OR PIE?

Strategy: Use a Graph

Problem solving with graphs makes information easier to analyze. Bar graphs are used to compare data. Line graphs are used to show a change in data over time. Pie graphs are used to compare pieces of information to the whole or to other pieces.

BAR GRAPH

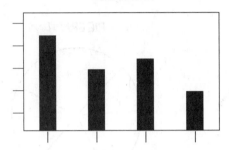

LINE GRAPH

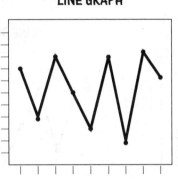

PIE GRAPH

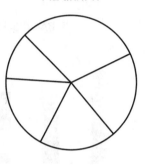

Try It! Identify which type of graph would best represent each set of information. Use *bar*, *line*, or *pie*.

1. Favorite flavors of ice cream by class members

_____

2. Daily science grades by all sixth graders for two weeks

_____

3. Monthly sales of movie tickets

_____

4. Time spent watching television in one week

_____

5. Daily average temperature for a month

_____

6. Favorite music groups by class members

_____

7. Percentage of budget used by each grade level for computers

_____

8. Votes received by 3 candidates in a school election

_____

Problem Solving Strategies 5, SV 0516-2

Name _____ Date _____

Unit 1 Review

. . . .
Strategy
• Use a Graph
. . . .

BAR GRAPH

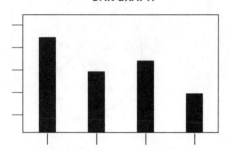

LINE GRAPH

PIE GRAPH

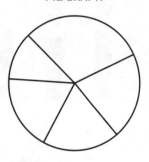

Show What You Know!

Identify which type of graph would best represent each set of information.

1. Average daily rainfall for your town in one month

_____

2. Percentage of glass, paper, metal, and plastic products a business recycles

_____

3. Number of birthdays during each month for students in your class

_____

4. Percentage of time you spend on homework, sports, and watching television after school

_____

5. The rate at which a plant grows each week for 12 weeks

_____

6. A taste test in which students classify and record the number of foods that taste sweet, salty, or sour

_____

Unit 1 Review, page 2

Show What You Know!

Use the graph to solve the problems.

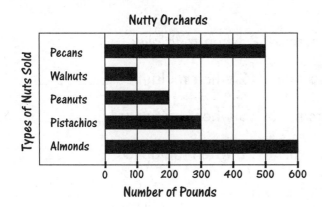

Nutty Orchards

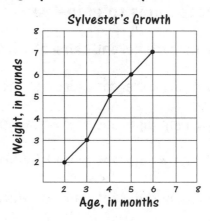

Sylvester's Growth

1. The Nutty Orchards sells 5 types of nuts. Which type of nut is most popular?

_____

2. Which type of nut is least popular?

_____

3. How many pounds of pistachios and peanuts were sold altogether?

_____

4. Tommy adopted a kitten named Sylvester from the local animal shelter. He used a line graph to keep track of Sylvester's weight. How much did Sylvester weigh when he was 2 months old?

_____

5. How old was Sylvester when he showed the greatest weight gain?

_____

6. How much weight had Sylvester gained from the time he was 2 months until he was 6 months?

_____

Extension

Locate a graph in a newspaper. Write 3 questions about the data shown in the graph. Trade the graph and questions with another student. Then answer each other's questions.

Name _____ Date _____

FLEX YOUR MATH MUSCLES

Flex is very confused by numbers sometimes. See if you can help him!

Name two whole numbers that make 17 when multiplied. _____

Use these clues to guide you.

1. How many different pairs of whole numbers make 8 when multiplied? _____

2. How many different pairs of whole numbers make 12 when multiplied? _____

3. How many different pairs of whole numbers make 16 when multiplied? _____

4. How many different pairs of whole numbers make 11 when multiplied? _____

5. How many different pairs of whole numbers make 13 when multiplied? _____

NUMBERS/FACTORS

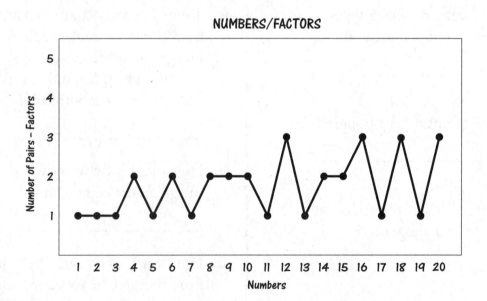

Use this graph to give Flex other examples of whole numbers that have only 1 pair of factors.

6. What are these numbers called? _____

7. Extend the graph for the whole numbers 21–30. What numbers have only 1 pair of

factors? _____

Problem Solving Strategies 5, SV 0516-2

Name _____ Date _____

LOOKING FOR CLUES

Strategy: Use Logic and Tables

Some problems can be solved with logic. Read the problem. Make a table. Look for clues to complete the table and solve the problem.

 Read the problem.
Jane, Jan, and June plan to meet at the library. One walks, one gets a ride from her father, and one rides the bus. Jane does not ride any vehicle. Jan's father does not have a car. Who walks? Who rides the bus? And who rides with her father?

 Make a table.
Show the names in a column at the left. Show what they may do across the top.

STEP 3 **Look for clues.**
Clue 1: Jane does not ride any vehicle. Use NO twice to show this in the table.

Clue 2: Jan's father does not have a car. Use a NO to show this in the table.

More clues: Use what is shown in the table. Since the row for Jane has 2 NOs, there must be a YES under Walk. Since the column for Car has 2 NOs, there must be a YES for June.

Since Jane walks and June rides with her father, Jan must take the bus.

	Walk	Bus	Car
Jane			
Jan			
June			

	Walk	Bus	Car
Jane		NO	NO
Jan			
June			

	Walk	Bus	Car
Jane		NO	NO
Jan			NO
June			

	Walk	Bus	Car
Jane	YES	NO	NO
Jan			NO
June			YES

	Walk	Bus	Car
Jane	YES	NO	NO
Jan	NO	YES	NO
June	NO	NO	YES

Unit 2, Logic
Problem Solving Strategies 5, SV 0516-2

Name _____ Date _____

CLUES ARE EVERYWHERE

Strategy: Use Logic and Tables

Try It!   Use logic and tables to solve the problems.

1. Ann, Beth, and Carl have pets. One has a dog, one has a hamster, and one has a canary. Ann is friends with the dog owner. Beth owns the hamster.

Who owns the canary? _____

Clue 1: Ann is friends with the dog owner, so she cannot be the dog owner. Put a NO for her under Dog.

Clue 2: Who gets a YES under hamster? _____

2. Yvonne, Jerry, and Elena finished first, second, and third in the spelling bee. Jerry was not first. Elena finished between the other two. Who finished first, who finished second, and who finished third?

1st _____   2nd _____   3rd _____

3. Donna, Linda, Sandi, and Nancy belong to different sports teams. One is on the swim team, one is on the softball team, one is on the basketball team, and one is on the track team. Sandi and Nancy are afraid of the water. Linda forgot her catcher's mitt at practice. Nancy won the 100-meter dash. Who is on which team?

_____   _____

_____   _____

_____   _____

Unit 2, Logic
Problem Solving Strategies 5, SV 0516-2

Name _____ Date _____

WORKING WITH CLUES THAT SEEM SKIMPY

Strategy: Use Logic and Tables

Sometimes the clues in a problem do not seem obvious. Read the problem carefully. Look for facts that are given to you. Make a table to organize the facts.

STEP 1 **Read the problem.**

A doctor, a lawyer, and an accountant work on the first, second, and third floors of an office building. The doctor goes upstairs every Friday to eat lunch with the accountant. The accountant goes downstairs to meet in the lawyer's office. The lawyer and the accountant ride the elevator to their offices. On what floor is each person's office?

STEP 2 **Make a table.**

	1st floor	2nd floor	3rd floor
Doctor			
Lawyer			
Accountant			

Try It! Use the clues to fill in the table.

1. One clue tells you the doctor goes upstairs to the accountant. This tells you that the doctor is not on the third floor and the accountant is not on the first floor.

2. Another clue tells you the accountant goes downstairs to the lawyer's office. This tells you that the accountant is not on the first floor and the lawyer is not on the third floor.

3. The last clue tells you that the lawyer and the accountant use the elevator to go to their offices. This tells you that neither has an office on the first floor.

4. On what floor is each person's office?

   doctor's office _____

   lawyer's office _____

   accountant's office _____

Problem Solving Strategies 5, SV 0516-2

Name _____ Date _____

LIFE ON THE STARSHIP PILGRIM

Strategy: Use Logic and Tables

Try It! Use logic and a table to find out who is who in this space story.

Adam, Sally, and Mario are among the crew on the starship *Pilgrim*. They wear different colored spacesuits.

Sally asks the astronaut in the white spacesuit to check the fuel tanks. Mario helps the astronaut in the green spacesuit to clean some juice stains off his suit.

What color spacesuit does each wear?

	White Suit	Green Suit	Blue Suit
Adam			
Sally			
Mario			

1. Adam wears a _____ spacesuit.

2. Sally wears a _____ spacesuit.

3. Mario wears a _____ spacesuit.

Problem Solving Strategies 5, SV 0516-2

Name _____   Date _____

THERE'S NO BUSINESS LIKE SHOW BUSINESS

Strategy: Use Logic and Tables

You know by now that logic means using your head. You look for clues in a story like a detective looks for clues in a mystery. You can organize the clues in a table. The table makes it easier to solve the problem.

 Read the problem.

Ms. Bernal, Mr. Peterson, Mr. Robinson, and Ms. Sorenson are very talented people. One is a dancer, one is a writer, one is a guitar player, and one is an artist. Ms. Bernal attended a concert given by the guitarist. Mr. Robinson also attended the same concert but did not go with Ms. Bernal. Both Mr. Peterson and the writer had their portraits painted by the artist. The writer has just finished writing a biography of Ms. Sorenson. The writer plans to write a biography of Ms. Bernal next. Ms. Bernal is not the artist. Who is the dancer, who is the writer, who is the guitarist, and who is the artist?

STEP 2 **Make a table to organize the clues.**

	Ms. Bernal	Mr. Peterson	Mr. Robinson	Ms. Sorenson
Dancer				
Writer				
Guitarist				
Artist				

Try It! Use the clues to fill in the table above and solve the problem.

1. The dancer is _____ .

2. The writer is _____ .

3. The guitarist is _____ .

4. The artist is _____ .

Problem Solving Strategies 5, SV 0516-2

WHO LIKES WHAT?

Strategy: Use Logic and Tables

Try It! Use logic and a table to solve the problem.

Sherry, Jerry, Merry, and Perry are all friends. One likes hamburgers, one likes spaghetti, one likes egg rolls, and one likes tacos.

Sherry likes ketchup on her favorite food. Merry always eats her favorite food with a fork. Perry adds toppings to his favorite food.

What is each friend's favorite food?

	Hamburgers	Spaghetti	Egg Rolls	Tacos
Sherry				
Jerry				
Merry				
Perry				

1. Sherry likes _____.

2. Jerry likes _____.

3. Merry likes _____.

4. Perry likes _____.

Problem Solving Strategies 5, SV 0516-2

MY DOG ATE MY HOMEWORK!

Strategy: Use Logic and Tables

Try It!   Use logic to solve the problem.

1. Four students, Anne, Brad, Chan, and Dana, all have favorite subjects in school. The different subjects are astronomy, chemistry, geography, and oceanography.

Dana does not use formulas nor a telescope in her favorite subject. Brad loves landforms and artifacts, but he does not like to swim. Chan does his class work only during the day.

	Astronomy	Chemistry	Geography	Oceanography
Anne				
Brad				
Chan				
Dana				

1. Anne's favorite is _____ .

2. Brad's favorite is _____ .

3. Chan's favorite is _____ .

4. Dana's favorite is _____ .

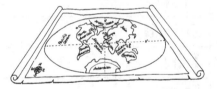

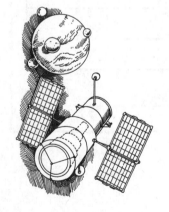

Problem Solving Strategies 5, SV 0516-2

Name _____ Date _____

Unit 2 Review

Strategies
- Use Logical Reasoning
- Use a Table

Show What You Know!

Use logical reasoning and a table to solve each problem.

1. There were 5 runners in a race. Anna came in first. Pete came in last. Tyrone was ahead of Katy. Ira was just behind Katy. Who won second place?

First	
Second	
Third	
Fourth	
Fifth	

_____

2. Darnell packed 5 boxes to ship to his grandparents in Michigan. Box A weighed the least. Box B weighed more than Box A but less than Box E. Box D weighed less than Box E but more than Box B. Box C weighed more than Box E. Which box was the heaviest?

5 (Heaviest)	
4	
3	
2	
1 (Lightest)	

_____

Unit 2, Logic
Problem Solving Strategies 5, SV 0516-2

Name _____ Date _____

Unit 2 Review, page 2

Strategies
- Use Logical Reasoning
- Use a Table

Show What You Know!

Use logical reasoning and a table to solve each problem.

1. A detective needed to solve the mystery of who stole a diamond ring. Five people had been in the house the night of the robbery. The detective knows that the ring was stolen at 8:15 P.M. because the crook broke a clock during the robbery. Mr. and Mrs. Sanders got home from the ballet at 10:00 P.M. Mr. Sanders left the house at 7:00 P.M. to meet his wife at the ballet. The delivery boy came to the house an hour before Mr. Sanders left. A man whose car had a flat tire came to the house before the Sanders came home but after the delivery boy had been there. A bird flew in an open window an hour after the man with the flat tire had been there. Who is the most likely suspect for stealing the ring?

10:00 P.M.	
9:00 P.M.	
8:00 P.M.	
7:00 P.M.	
6:00 P.M.	

_____

2. Shameka, Wendy, Caleb, and Arturo each play an instrument in the school band. The instruments they play are the violin, tuba, drums, and flute.

Caleb's instrument has strings. Shameka's does not have strings nor does it have a mouthpiece. Wendy's instrument is easy to carry. Arturo's instrument is the biggest one.

	Violin	Tuba	Drums	Flute
Shameka				
Wendy				
Caleb				
Arturo				

Shameka plays the _____.   Caleb plays the _____.

Wendy plays the _____.   Arturo plays the _____.

Problem Solving Strategies 5, SV 0516-2

Name _____ Date _____

Flex wanted a different way to solve logic problems. He used Venn diagrams of overlapping circles.

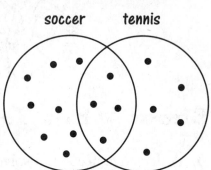

Sample:

At your school, 12 students play soccer. 9 students play tennis. 4 students play both sports. How many play only 1 sport?

___13 students___

Try to use Flex's method to solve these problems. Use either dots or numbers in the diagrams.

1

At a track meet, 22 students ran in the 100-meter race. 15 students ran in the 200-meter race. 6 students ran in both races. How many ran in at least one race?

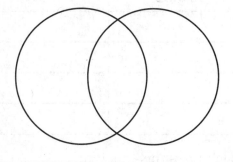

_____

2

15 students tried out for the swimming team. 12 tried out for the track team. 10 tried out for both teams. How many students tried out for only one team?

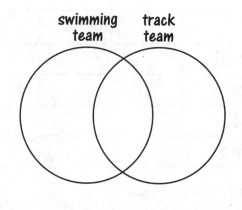

_____

Problem Solving Strategies 5, SV 0516-2

Name _____ Date _____

TOO MUCH INFORMATION

Strategy: Identify Extra Information

Sometimes a problem gives too much information. Read the problem. Underline the information you need. Cross out the information you do not need. Solve the problem.

 Read the problem.
Jeff saves $155 to buy a new bike. A new bike costs $125. A used bike costs $75. How much more does a new bike cost than a used one?

STEP 2 **Underline what you need. Cross out what you do not need.**
~~Jeff saves $155 to buy a new bike.~~ <u>A new bike costs $125. A used bike costs $75.</u> How much more does a new bike cost than a used one?

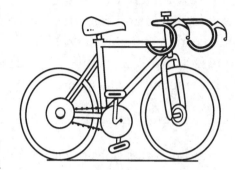

STEP 3 **Subtract. Solve the problem.**
$125 − $75 = $50
A new bike costs $50 more.

Try It! Underline what you need. Cross out what you do not need. Solve the problems.

1. Your mother goes to the store. She has $25. She gives the clerk a $20 bill. He gives her $9.50 change. How much did your mother spend?

_____

2. Your brother is selling cookie dough containers for $4 each. He has sold 25 containers. He needs to sell a total of 86 to win a prize. How many more containers does he need to sell to win a prize?

_____

3. Your father buys 8.5 gallons of gas. He also buys 1 quart of oil for $1.75. Gas costs $1.40 per gallon. How much did your father spend for gas?

_____

4. Your sister buys dog food once a month. She feeds the dog 112 ounces of dog food each week. How many ounces per day is this?

_____

Problem Solving Strategies 5, SV 0516-2

Name _____ Date _____

CROSS OUT THE EXTRA STUFF

Strategy: Identify Extra Information

When a problem has too much information, cross out what you do not need. Use the other information to solve the problem.

Try It! Cross out what you do not need. Use the rest to solve the problems.

1. The Disk Depot is having a half-price sale on CDs and cassettes. You buy some CDs. You give the clerk $20. The sales tax is $0.96. You receive $2.85 change. How much do you spend?

_____

2. Anthony walks dogs to earn money. He walks 4 dogs in the morning and 6 dogs in the evening. Each owner pays him 50 cents per walking. How much does Anthony earn each morning?

_____

3. Julio spent $6 on a present for his father, $2 for a card, and $2 for wrapping paper. He also bought 3 books for $3 each. How much did Julio spend on his father?

_____

4. Nadia has a full-time job during summer vacation. She earns $5.25 per hour. She works 40 hours a week. She saves $100 from her pay. How much does she earn each week?

_____

5. Gina jogs for an hour every morning before school. She jogs between 2 and 3 miles every school day. How many hours does she jog during a school week?

_____

6. Tina practices the piano for 30 minutes on the 5 weekdays. She practices for 60 minutes every Saturday and Sunday. How many minutes does Tina spend practicing the piano Monday through Friday?

_____

ABOUT HOW MUCH?

Strategy: Use Estimation

To estimate a sum, round each number to the same place. Then add.

 STEP 1 **Read the problem.**
Jon has 64 country CDs and 37 rock CDs. About how many CDs does he have in all?

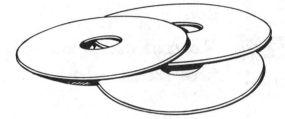

STEP 2 **Round each number to the same place.**
64 → 60
37 → 40

STEP 3 **Add. Solve the problem.**
60 + 40 = 100. He has about 100 CDs.

Try It! Round the numbers to the same place. Then estimate to solve the problems.

1. The Music Barn serves 1,112 customers on Friday. It serves 1,555 on Saturday. About how many customers does the Barn serve on both days?

   _____

2. The Squeaky Wheels play a two-night concert. The first night 72,744 fans attend. The second night 58,922 fans attend. About how many fans attend both nights?

   _____

3. Heather sold popcorn at the concert for $2.75 a bag. She sold 9,981 bags the first night. About how much money did she make the first night?

   _____

4. The Music Barn sells 272 copies of a new rock CD the first day. It sells 312 the next day. About how many copies does the Barn sell both days?

   _____

5. Jackie takes photographs of the concert for the newspaper. She takes 137 photos the first night and 189 the second night. About how many photos does she take both nights?

   _____

6. Ricardo buys 3 CDs at the Music Barn. The CDs cost $11.99, $13.10, and $17.99. About how much does he spend?

   _____

Name _____ Date _____

WHAT'S THE DIFFERENCE?

Strategy: Use Estimation

To estimate a difference, round each number to the same place. Then subtract.

STEP 1 **Read the problem.**
Koyi has 212 photos. Harua has 94. About how many more photos does Koyi have?

STEP 2 **Round each number to the same place.**
212 → 200
94 → 100

STEP 3 **Subtract. Solve the problem.**
200 − 100 = 100. Koyi has about 100 more photos.

Try It! Round the numbers to the same place. Then estimate to solve the problems.

1. Rita plants 28 bushes on a sunny day. She plants only 12 bushes on a rainy day. About how many more bushes does she plant on the sunny day?

_____

2. A jet plane can fly 870 mph with a tail wind. It can fly only 410 mph with a head wind. About how much faster can it fly with a tail wind?

_____

3. Mrs. Acosta raises bees to produce honey. During the summer, one beehive produces 108 pounds of honey. Another beehive produces 22 pounds. About how much more honey does the first hive produce than the second?

_____

4. Birmingham, AL, is 1,052 miles from Boston, MA, and 581 miles from Dallas, TX. About how much farther is it from Birmingham to Boston than it is to Dallas?

_____

5. Toronto is the largest city in Canada with a population of 4,682,897. Ottawa is the capital and has a population of 1,063,664. About how many more people are in Toronto?

_____

6. Mr. Chang used 145 gallons of gas in his truck in September and 158 gallons in October. About how much more gas did he use in October than in September?

_____

Name _____ Date _____

CHOOSE ONE OR THE OTHER

Strategy: Choose an Operation

Sometimes you must choose whether to add or subtract to solve a problem. Look for what the problem asks you to do. If it asks you to put together or join groups, then you usually add. If it asks you to take away or compare groups, then you usually subtract.

STEP 1 Read the problem.
Lee and Pat are potting plants to sell in their plant shop. Lee puts 36 geraniums in pots. Pat puts 60 daisies in pots. How many plants in all do they put into pots?

STEP 2 Look for what the problem asks you to do.
It asks you to put together two groups of plants. So, you add.

STEP 3 Add. Solve the problem.
36 + 60 = 96. They put 96 plants into pots.

Try It! Decide whether to add or subtract. Then solve the problems.

1. There are 54 marigold plants, 68 zinnia plants, and 49 petunia plants in one part of the plant shop. How many plants in all are in this part?

   _____

2. Lionel puts 48 more geraniums in pots for the sale. Together with the 36 he already potted, how many geraniums does the plant shop have to sell now?

   _____

3. The plant shop has a special holiday sale. During the sale, they sell 25 of their 54 marigold plants. How many marigold plants do they have left?

   _____

4. Pauline moves the 49 petunia plants into the front part of the shop. By the end of the day, 28 are sold. How many petunia plants are left to sell?

   _____

MELBORP EHT DAER

Strategy: Work Backward

When you know how things turn out but not how they started, you just might have to work backward. Look for clues as you read the problem.

 Read the problem.

Mike has 35 comic books. Dolores has 25 comic books. Last week Mike traded 8 of his comic books to Dolores for 5 of hers. How many comic books did Mike have before the trade?

STEP 2 Look for clues.

Clue 1: Mike has 35 comic books now.
Clue 2: He gave 8 comic books to Dolores.
Clue 3: He got 5 comic books from Dolores.

STEP 3 Work backward. Solve the problem.

Subtract the comic books he got from Dolores.
$35 - 5 = 30$
Add the comic books he gave to Dolores.
$30 + 8 = 38$
Mike had 38 comic books before the trade.

Try It! Work backward. Then solve the problems.

1. Barney gives 8 trading cards to his brother. He gives 6 to his sister. He has 45 cards left. How many did he begin with?

_____

2. Siva trades 8 space cards to get 5 from Kim. Then she buys 10 more. She has 98 cards now. How many did she begin with?

_____

3. Carlos trades 12 comic books for 8 of Jan's. He trades 5 for 6 of Pete's. He has 20 books now. How many did he begin with?

_____

4. Maria has 37 seashells. This is after she bought 5 and gave 8 to her brother. How many did she begin with?

_____

TAKE IT ONE STEP AT A TIME

Strategy: Identify Substeps

Sometimes a problem requires more than one step to solve. Just organize the facts you know. Then take one step at a time.

STEP 1 **Read the problem.**
Compustore has 75 computers in stock. On Monday they sell 8. On Tuesday they sell 6. How many computers do they have left to sell?

STEP 2 **Organize the facts.**
The store has 75 computers.
They sell 8. Then they sell 6.

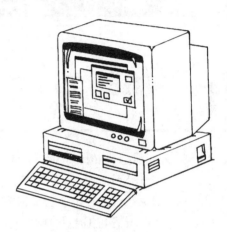

STEP 3 **Work the substeps.**
Solve the problem.
Add to find how many they sell.
$8 + 6 = 14$
Subtract to find how many they have left.
$75 - 14 = 61$
They have 61 computers left to sell.

Try It! Look for the facts. Then take it one step at a time to solve the problems.

1. Armando saves $1,000 to buy a computer. He buys one for $895. The sales tax is $53.70. How much money does Armando have left?

_____

2. Jeanine buys a box of computer paper for $9.95, a magazine for $1.95, and disks for $6.99. She pays with a $20 bill. How much change does she get?

_____

3. Helene and Hank share a box of 100 computer disks. She has used 21 disks, and he has used 27 disks. How many computer disks do they have left?

_____

4. Angela wants a printer that costs $175.95. She has saved $85.37. She has earned $48.25 working part time. How much more money does she need?

_____

Unit 3 Review

Strategies

- Identify Extra Information
- Use Estimation
- Choose an Operation
- Work Backward
- Identify Substeps

Show What You Know!

Solve each problem. Identify the strategy you used.

1. Mrs. Daniels bought $12.57 worth of gas. She gave the clerk $20.00. When she put the change in her wallet, she had a total of $43.00. How much change did Mrs. Daniels get from the clerk?

_____

2. Victor had a model airplane collection. He bought some of the planes by saving his allowance and doing chores for neighbors. His father gave him 3 planes, his aunt gave him 2 planes, and his sister gave him 1 plane. He now has 14 planes in his collection. How many model planes did Victor pay for himself?

_____

3. Pun travels 27 miles to visit her grandparents. She has to go another 16 miles if she wants to visit her aunt and uncle. About how far does she have to travel to visit her aunt and uncle?

_____

4. Nadine has a small bookshelf in her bedroom. She put 12 books on the first shelf and 16 books on the second shelf. Her brother borrowed 4 books from the first shelf and 2 books from the second shelf. How many books are still on Nadine's shelf?

_____

5. Pierre earned 31 points in the first round of a board game. He earned another 48 points during the second round. About how many points did he earn during the 2 rounds?

_____

Unit 3 Review, page 2

Show What You Know!

Solve each problem. Reduce your answer if possible. Identify the strategy you used.

1. Patty measured the rainfall at her house. It rained 12 inches in May, 17 inches in June, 15 inches in July, and 8 inches in August. How many inches did it rain during the 4 months? Did you add or subtract to solve the problem?

_____

2. Lola made friendship bracelets by stringing colorful beads together. She gave 8 bracelets to friends at school. She gave 5 bracelets to friends in her Girl Scout Troop. She still has 4 bracelets left to give to her friends in her neighborhood. How many bracelets did Lola make for her friends?

_____

3. Mr. Sánchez was born in 1921. He got married in 1946. He had his first grandchild in 1985. How old was Mr. Sánchez when his first grandchild was born?

_____

4. Frank bought 12 tickets for the Lee School Talent Show. He gave all the tickets away to friends. He bought and gave away 7 more tickets. Then 3 friends found out that they could not go to the show, so they returned the tickets to Frank. How many tickets were used by Frank's friends?

_____

Extension ....

Look at a biography for a famous person in history, such as Martin Luther King, Jr. Subtract the year of death from the year of birth to find out how old the person was when he or she died.

Problem Solving Strategies 5, SV 0516-2

Name _____ Date _____

FLEX YOUR MATH MUSCLES

1

Think of an even number of 1 or 2 digits. Write it here. _____

Double your number. _____

Add 12. _____

Divide by 4. _____

Take half of your original number.

_____

Subtract the above number from the last total. _____

Write your answer. _____

2

Think of a whole number. Write it here. _____

Double your number. _____

Add 6. _____

Divide by 2. _____

Subtract your number. _____

Write your answer. _____

3

Try some other numbers with each set of directions. Is 3 always the answer? How is it possible to predict the answer? You can figure it out. [Hint: Each step you do is undone later in the directions.]

Problem Solving Strategies 5, SV 0516-2

HAPPY BIRTHDAY TO YOU

Strategy: Choose an Operation

Sometimes you must decide what operation to use to solve a problem. Look for the action. Joining usually means you add or multiply. Taking away or comparing usually means you subtract or divide.

STEP 1 ▷ Read the problem.
Tomorrow is Katrina's birthday. She hung 15 balloons in each corner of the square family room. How many balloons did she hang in all?

STEP 2 ▷ Choose an operation.
Look for key words to help you decide which operation to use. The words *in all* signal addition or multiplication. To find how many in all, you join the 4 equal sets of balloons.

STEP 3 ▷ Add or multiply. Solve the problem.
$15 + 15 + 15 + 15 = 60$ or $4 \times 15 = 60$
She hung 60 balloons in all.

Try It! Choose the correct operation to solve the problems.

1. Katrina sets 12 plates around the table for her guests. If she places 6 tiny prizes on each plate, how many prizes will she need in all?

   _____

2. Katrina places 4 candy dishes on the table. She has 12 small candies for each dish. How many candies does she have in all?

   _____

3. Katrina spent 30 minutes a day for 5 days planning the party. How many minutes in all did she spend planning?

   _____

4. During the party Katrina and her guests choose partners to play a game. If there are 6 pairs of partners, how many people are there?

   _____

5. After the party, Katrina thanks 11 guests for their gifts. She thanks each guest 3 times. How many times in all did Katrina thank her guests?

   _____

6. Eight of Katrina's friends took balloons home. If each friend took 7 balloons, how many balloons in all did they take?

   _____

TRADE YOU TWO OF THESE FOR ONE OF THOSE

Strategy: Identify Substeps

Sometimes you need to use more than one operation to solve a problem.

STEP 1 ▷ **Read the problem.**

Phyllis has a collection of 72 trading cards. She goes to a card collectors' show and buys 5 sets of cards. There are 12 cards in each set. How many cards does she have now?

STEP 2 ▷ **Decide what the problem asks.**

The problem asks how many cards she has now.

STEP 3 ▷ **Identify the substeps.**

Substep 1: Multiply to find how many cards she bought.

Substep 2: Add the number of cards she bought to the number she already has to find how many she has now.

STEP 4 ▷ **Work the substeps. Solve the problem.**

She buys 5 sets of 12 cards. $5 \times 12 = 60$
She adds these to her other cards. $60 + 72 = 132$
She has 132 cards.

Try It! Identify the substeps and choose the operation. Solve the problems.

1. Philip trades 3 sets of football cards for 5 sets of hockey cards. There are 10 cards in each set of football cards. There are 8 cards in each set of hockey cards. How many more cards did Philip have after the trade?

2. Phyllis makes sets of 4 with her 44 duplicate cards. Philip makes sets of 5 with his 55 duplicate cards. Phyllis trades 6 of her sets for 5 of Philip's sets. Who gets more cards and how many more?

IF I HAD A HAMMER

Strategy: Guess and Check

A way to solve some problems is to guess the answer. Make a guess. Then check it. Use what you learn from the first guess to guess again.

 Read the problem.

Jorge's woodworking book is open. If the product of the page numbers is 506, what are the page numbers?

STEP 2 Decide what you know.

The pages are facing pages, so the numbers are consecutive numbers. One is even and one is odd.

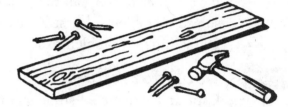

STEP 3 Guess and check until you find the answer.

Guess 1: 16×17 **Check:** $16 \times 17 = 272$ **Result:** Too small

Guess 2: 26×27 **Check:** $26 \times 27 = 702$ **Result:** Too great

Guess 3: 22×23 **Check:** $22 \times 23 = 506$ **Result:** Just right

The book is open to pages 22 and 23.

Try It! Guess and check to solve the problems.

1. Jorge is 1 year older than Julia. The product of their ages is 240. How old is each?

_____ _____

2. Jorge's sister Julia builds a wagon for their little brother. She spends $40 for wood and wheels. The wood costs $2 more than the wheels. How much did the wood cost?

_____

3. Jorge flips to two other pages in the book. The product of the page numbers is 210. What are the page numbers?

_____ _____

4. Jorge buys a hammer and a saw. Altogether they cost $48. The hammer costs $6 more than the saw. What is the cost of each?

_____ _____

BACK IT UP

Strategy: Work Backward

Sometimes you have to work backward to solve a problem. Look for clues to help you.

STEP 1 **Read the problem.**

The math teacher assigns each student a different set of problems. The students all get the same number of problems. There are 24 students in class. Students have 1 hour to solve all the problems. By the middle of the hour, Henrik had solved 6 problems. He still has 10 more to solve by the end of the hour. How many different problems did the math teacher assign?

STEP 2 **Look for clues.**

Clue 1: There are 24 students in class. Each is assigned the same number of problems.

Clue 2: Henrik has solved 6 problems and still has 10 more to do.

STEP 3 **Work backward. Solve the problem.**

Add to find the number of problems Henrik must solve. $6 + 10 = 16$
Multiply to find the total numbers of problems. $16 \times 24 = 384$
The math teacher assigned 384 different problems.

Try It! Work backward. Look for clues. Solve the problems.

1. The materials secretary made photocopies of problem pages for all 180 students in school. Each student got the same number of pages. Kim has completed 8 pages and has 2 more to do. How many pages in all did the secretary make?

   _____

2. At the store, Gino bought a pack of nuts for $0.50 and 2 whistles for $0.35 each. If he receives $0.80 in change, how much money did he give the cashier in the store?

   _____

3. Sophie has 25 problems to do. She did 6 yesterday. Today she did half as many problems as she did yesterday. Tomorrow she will do 4 times as many as she did today. How many problems will she still have to do after tomorrow?

   _____

4. Luther's scout troop is on a 3-day hiking trip. They will cover 32 miles. On the first day, they hiked 8 miles. On the second day, they hiked twice as many miles as on the first day. How many miles will they have to hike on the third day?

   _____

Name _____ Date _____

TALES FROM OUT OF THIS WORLD

Strategy: Identify Extra or Missing Information

Some problems give too many facts. Some problems do not give enough facts. Can you tell when you have too many or not enough facts?

STEP 1 ▶ **Read the problem.**
There are 11 countries on the planet Zanzan. Each country has 1,111 Zanzanians. 7,221 Zanzanians live on the northern continent. How many Zanzanians live on the planet?

STEP 2 ▶ **Identify what the problem asks you to find.**
How many Zanzanians live on Zanzan?

STEP 3 ▶ **Identify the facts.**
There are 11 countries on the planet Zanzan. Each country has 1,111 Zanzanians.

STEP 4 ▶ **Identify extra or missing facts.**
Extra fact: 7,221 Zanzanians live on the northern continent.

 Try It! Identify the extra or missing facts.

1. Space Cadet Kimta travels 5,678 light-years to Alpha Galaxy. Her next flight will take her 8 times farther. Alpha and Beta galaxies are 3,657 light-years apart. How many light-years will Cadet Kimta travel on her next flight?

_____

2. The spaceship *Dauntless* takes off at 2:00 A.M. on January 5, 2125. It carries a crew of 1,500 space cadets, regulars, and officers. Its destination is Gamma Galaxy. What time will the *Dauntless* arrive in Gamma Galaxy?

_____

TALES FROM OUT OF THIS WORLD, part 2

Strategy: Identify Extra or Missing Information

Some problems give one or more extra facts. Some problems do not give enough facts. Can you tell when you have too many or not enough facts?

Try It! Cross out extra facts. If there are not enough facts, tell what fact or facts are missing.

1. There are 98 Golphinians waiting to begin their courses at the Space Academy. Altogether, the Academy can train 7 times this number of students. Last year, there were 500 students enrolled in the Academy. How many students can the Academy train at one time?

_____

_____

_____

2. The space freighter *Ulysses* has 548 barrels of gemstones loaded in it. Captain Quitebright ordered the cargo master to load 20 times this number of barrels. How much will this number of barrels of gemstones be worth?

_____

_____

_____

3. The Jessians have mined 313 tons of ore so far this year. They have orders for 25 times that many tons of ore. The King of Jesse has all the ore shipped to the planet Moondog. How many space freighters are needed to take the ore from Jesse to Moondog?

_____

_____

_____

4. This year, 978 Merkians traveled to the planet Patooie. A Merkian travel agency reported that 150 times that many Merkians traveled during the last 15 years. How many Merkians traveled only to the planet Patooie during the last 15 years?

_____

_____

_____

Name _____ Date _____

ON A BICYCLE BUILT FOR TWO

Strategy: Use Estimation

There are times when you do not need an exact answer to solve a problem. You can estimate by rounding the numbers before computing.

 Read the problem.

Kevin sells 63 bicycles. Each bicycle sells for about $190. To win a trip to Hawaii, Kevin must sell $10,000 worth of bikes. Has he done this yet?

 Identify the facts you need.

63 bicycles sold. Each sells for about $190. Need at least $10,000.

 Round the numbers and estimate to solve the problem.

63 is about 60. $190 is about $200. 60 × $200 = $12,000. Kevin has reached his goal.

Try It! Round the numbers. Then estimate to solve the problems.

1. There were 22 tandem bikes, 13 dirt bikes, and 78 regular bikes in the bike marathon. Tandem bikes have 2 riders. Dirt and regular bikes have 1 rider. About how many riders were in the bike marathon?

_____

2. 616 bike riders finished the 12-mile route to raise money for charity. Each earned 20¢ a mile. About how much did all the riders raise for charity?

_____

3. Last year, a total of 15,978 people from the Northeast joined a bike safety program. At least 3 times that many joined from the Midwest. About how many people from the Midwest joined the program?

_____

4. There are 26 schools in Center City. Each school has 4 bike racks. Each rack holds 18 bikes. About how many bikes in all fit into the racks?

_____

Unit 4 Review

Show What You Know!

Solve each problem. Identify the strategy you used.

1. Both Lee and Clay are growing a plant. Lee's plant is 4 inches taller than Clay's plant. The product of their heights is 32 inches. How tall is each plant?

_____

_____

2. Ms. Cantrell was going to decorate a bulletin board for her kindergarten class. She made 2 copies of 26 letters of the alphabet on blue paper. She has already put 17 letters on the bulletin board. How many more letters does she need to put on it?

_____

3. A department store has a shoe display. There are 24 pairs of shoes on each of the 4 lower shelves and 15 pairs of shoes on each of 4 upper shelves. About how many pairs of shoes are shown in the display?

_____

4. Ted is a salesman and has taken 8 trips to different foreign countries this year. He has 2 more countries to visit. He visits the same countries every year. He has taken a total of 50 trips. How many years has he been making these trips?

_____

Unit 4 Review, page 2

Strategies

- Choose an Operation
- Identify Substeps
- Guess and Check
- Work Backward
- Identify Extra or Missing Information
- Use Estimation

Show What You Know!

Solve each problem. Identify the strategy you used.

1. Priscilla bought 3 packages of pencils. Each pencil cost 7 cents. How much did Priscilla spend on the pencils?

_____

2. Gary bought 4 sacks of potatoes for his restaurant. Each sack weighed 10 pounds. How many pounds of potatoes did Gary buy?

_____

3. Zeba bought 8 dolls for $4.00 each and 3 dolls for $2.00 each. She gave the store clerk $40. How much change did she get?

_____

4. Quinn read 3 times as many pages of a magazine as Tonya. Christa read 20 pages, and Tonya read 6 pages. How many pages did Quinn read?

_____

5. Candy walked 2 miles more on Tuesday than she did on Monday. The product of distance that Candy walked is 8 miles. How many miles did Candy walk each day?

_____

_____

Extension

Count the number of students in your class. Count the number of textbooks each student has. What is the total number of textbooks that have been distributed to the entire class?

FLEX YOUR MATH MUSCLES

1

Flex goes panning for gold in the mountains. Lucky Flex finds gold. In fact, he finds quite a bit of gold. He wonders how much it is worth. He sees in the morning paper that gold is worth $367.95 an ounce that day. If Flex had a pound of gold, how much would it be worth?

_____

2

Of course, Flex does not think he has a pound of gold. He reaches into his backpack for his balance scale to weigh the gold. He discovers that he forgot to bring weights for the scale. But he finds that he did bring a 1-pound bar of chocolate candy. What if he cuts the bar into 2 equal pieces? What can he tell about how much gold he has?

_____

_____

3

What if Flex cuts the candy bar into 4 equal pieces? Now what can he tell about his gold?

_____

_____

4

Actually the candy bar was marked off in 1-ounce pieces, but he had eaten a piece while pondering his problem. How can he use the remaining 15 pieces to find how much gold he has?

_____

_____

5

At last Flex finds that he has 12 ounces of gold. At $367.95 an ounce, how much did Flex make for all his troubles?

_____

_____

Name _____ Date _____

HERE'S FOOD FOR THOUGHT

Strategy: Identify Substeps; Choose an Operation

Sometimes you need to use more than one operation to solve a problem. When you must choose the operation, look at the action involved. Joining equal groups usually means multiplication. Separating into equal groups or comparing usually means division.

STEP 1 ▷ Read the problem.

Pam had to slice 100 carrots for a party. She made 8 carrot sticks from each carrot. She arranged the carrot sticks evenly on 20 trays. How many carrot sticks were on each tray?

STEP 2 ▷ Identify the substeps.

Substep 1: Multiply to find how many carrot sticks there are.
Substep 2: Divide to find how many carrot sticks were on each tray.

STEP 3 ▷ Work the substeps. Solve the problem.

She has 100 equal sets of 8 carrot sticks. $100 \times 8 = 800$
She separates 800 into equal sets of 20. $800 \div 20 = 40$
There are 40 carrot sticks on each tray.

Try It! Identify the substeps and choose the operations to solve the problems.

1. Chung has 3 ten-pound bags of potatoes. In each bag there are 24 potatoes. He peels half the potatoes for Thanksgiving dinner. How many potatoes did Chung peel?

_____

2. Bo needs to buy 3 granola bars. At the store, Bo sees Block brand bars, which cost 93¢ for a package of 3 bars. Bo also sees Wells brand bars, which cost 25¢ each. Which bars are less expensive? How much less expensive are they?

_____

_____

3. Jenny's Gifts buys 18 crates of peaches with 54 peaches in each. Jenny uses 6 peaches to make a fruit basket. How many baskets can she make?

_____

4. Santos is buying oranges. At one store, the oranges are 96¢ for a half dozen. Another store is selling oranges for 20¢ each. Which is the better deal?

_____

Name _____ Date _____

THE HUSTLE AND BUSTLE OF EVERYDAY LIFE

Strategy: Identify Substeps

Some problems require more than one step to solve. Just look for what the problem asks and then use the facts to solve it.

 STEP 1 ▷ Read the problem.
Manuel buys 3 loaves of bread for $3.39, 4 pounds of fruit for $4.04, and 2 gallons of milk for $5.78. How much less would he spend if he bought only 1 loaf of bread, 1 pound of fruit, and 1 gallon of milk?

STEP 2 ▷ Identify the substeps.
Substep 1: First find how much he spends.
Substep 2: Then find how much he would have spent for 1 of each item.
Substep 3: Then find the difference.

STEP 3 ▷ Solve the problem.
Find how much Manuel spends. $3.39 + $4.04 + $5.78 = $13.21
Find how much he would have spent for 1 of each.
$3.39 ÷ 3 = $1.13, $4.40 ÷ 4 = $1.10, $5.78 ÷ 2 = $2.89
$1.13 + $1.10 + $2.89 = $5.12
Find the difference. $13.21 − $5.12 = $8.09
Manuel would have spent $8.09 less.

Try It! Identify the substeps and choose the operations to solve the problems.

1. There are 735 residences in Ashland. Each mail route covers 245 residences. There are 432 residences in Shelby. Each mail route covers 108 residences. How many mail routes are there altogether in Ashland and Shelby?

_____

2. A work crew must install 640 windows in a 32-story building. Each floor has 4 offices. Each office has the same number of windows. It takes 2 hours to install 1 window. How long will it take the crew to install all the windows in 1 office?

_____

Problem Solving Strategies 5, SV 0516-2

FAMILY PHOTO ALBUMS

Strategy: Guess and Check

One way to solve certain problems is to guess. Then check your guess. Keep guessing and checking until you find the answer.

STEP 1 ▷ **Read the problem.**

The number of pages in the family photo album is a 2-digit number. The number of photos on a page is a 1-digit number. The number of pages is 40 more than the number of photos on a page. The number of pages divided by the number of photos on a page is 6. What is the number of pages in the album?

STEP 2 ▷ **Decide what you know.**

The number of pages is a 2-digit number.
The number of photos on a page is a 1-digit number.
The number of pages is 40 more than the number of photos on a page.
The number of pages divided by the number of photos is 6.

STEP 3 ▷ **Guess and check until you find the answer.**

Guess 1: 49 and 9   **Check:** $49 \div 9 < 6$
Guess 2: 44 and 4   **Check:** $44 \div 4 > 6$
Guess 3: 48 and 8   **Check:** $48 \div 8 = 6$
There are 48 pages in the album.

Try It!   Guess and check to solve the problems.

1. The number of pages is a 2-digit number. The number of photos on a page is a 1-digit number. The number of pages is 60 more than the number of photos on a page. The number of pages divided by the number of photos on a page is 16. What is the number of pages?

2. The number of pages is a 2-digit number. The number of photos on a page is a 1-digit number. The number of pages is 90 more than the number of photos on each. The number of pages divided by the number of photos on each is 11. What is the number of pages?

FISHING AT THE FAIR

Strategy: Work Backward

Sometimes you need to work backward to solve a problem.

 Read the problem.

Ron must order flags for the school fair. He knows that 144 flags come in a carton. There are 6 booths at the fair, and each booth requires 48 flags. How many cartons should Ron order?

 Look for clues.

Clue 1: There are 144 flags in a carton.
Clue 2: There are 6 booths at the fair.
Clue 3: A booth requires 48 flags.

STEP 3 Work backward. Solve the problem.

Find how many flags are needed for all the booths.

$6 \times 48 = 288$

Then find the number of cartons that have this many flags.

$288 \div 144 = 2$

Ron must order 2 cartons.

Try It! Work backward to solve the problems.

1. Ann, Ben, Cara, and Dee make prizes for the fair. Ben makes twice as many prizes as Ann. Cara makes 14 fewer than Ben and half as many as Dee. Dee makes 60 prizes. How many do Ann, Ben, and Cara make?

_____

_____

_____

2. Ann spends $1.00 for a hot dog and 40¢ for a soda. How much money did she start with if she has $3.60 left?

_____

3. Rosa sells 16 tickets for the fair. Gina sells 4 times as many tickets as Rolando. Rolando sells 12 tickets. How many tickets in all did Rosa, Gina, and Rolando sell altogether?

_____

4. Jon spends $2.20 for a ticket, and $1.40 each for a sandwich and a super cola. He has $5.00 left. How much did he start with?

_____

Name _____ Date _____

INTO THE WILD BLUE YONDER

Strategy: Use Estimation

There are times when you do not need an exact number to solve a problem. You can estimate. One way to estimate is to round numbers.

 Read the problem.
The jumbo jet flew 17,870 miles last week. It made 62 flights. About how many miles did the jet fly on each flight?

STEP 2 Identify what the problem asks.
About how many miles did the jet fly on each flight?

STEP 3 Round the numbers and estimate to solve the problem.
You should divide 17,870 by 62, but the word *about* tells you that an estimate will be sufficient.
17,870 is about 18,000. 62 is about 60. 18,000 ÷ 60 = 300
It flew about 300 miles on each flight.

Try It! Round the numbers. Then estimate to solve the problems.

1. To earn her pilot's license, Kahva must fly 19,927 miles. She plans 38 flights. About how many miles must she fly on each flight?

_____

2. The same number of planes use the Kookytown airport everyday. During 22 days, 1,898 planes used the airport. About how many planes used the airport each day?

_____

3. Flight 912 covers 30,284 miles and makes 63 stops. If the distances between stops are almost equal, about what is the distance between 2 stops?

_____

4. 819 people visit the air show where a special plane is on display. If 41 people can view the plane at a time, how many groups would enable everyone at the air show to see the plane?

_____

Problem Solving Strategies 5, SV 0516-2

LUNCH TIME

Strategy: Make a Table

Sometimes a problem has so many facts, you should make a table to organize the facts. The table will make it easier to solve the problem.

 Read the problem.

Don and Dana own a sandwich shop. Each day they offer sandwich specials. On Monday, they have 3 specials: ham on French rolls, turkey on wheat rolls, and meatballs on sesame rolls. They use 150 slices of ham, 180 slices of turkey, and 90 meatballs. They also use 25 French rolls, 30 wheat rolls, and 15 sesame rolls. How many pieces of meat did they use for each kind of sandwich?

STEP 2 **List the facts you need.**

Fact 1: Ham on French, turkey on wheat, and meatballs on sesame rolls
Fact 2: 150 slices of ham, 180 slices of turkey, 90 meatballs
Fact 3: 25 French rolls, 30 wheat rolls, 15 sesame rolls

STEP 3 **Organize the facts in a table.**

		French rolls	Wheat rolls	Sesame rolls
		25	30	15
Ham slices	150	$150 \div 25 = 6$		
Turkey slices	180		$180 \div 30 = 6$	
Meatballs	90			$90 \div 15 = 6$

 Read the table. Solve the problem.

They used 6 pieces of meat for each sandwich.

Try It! Use the table to help you solve the problem.

1. On Tuesday, Don and Dana have 3 specials: ham on wheat rolls, turkey on sesame rolls, and meatballs on French rolls. They use 150 slices of ham, 180 slices of turkey, and 100 meatballs. They also use 25 French rolls, 30 wheat rolls, and 15 sesame rolls. How many pieces of meat did they use for each kind of sandwich?

Name _____   Date _____

LUNCH TIME, part 2

Strategy: Make a Table

Sometimes a problem has so many facts, you should make a table to
organize the facts. The table will make it easier to solve the problem.

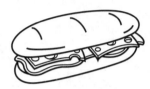

Try It! Make a table to help you solve the problems.

1. On Thursday, Don and Dana make these specials: ham on sesame roll, turkey on French
roll, and meatballs on wheat roll. They use 150 slices of ham, 180 slices of turkey, and
90 meatballs. They have 30 wheat rolls, 30 French rolls, and 15 sesame rolls. How many
pieces of meat should they use for each sandwich?

_____

2. Over the weekend, Don and Dana's Sandwich Shop sold 94 ham sandwiches, 100 turkey
sandwiches, and 82 meatball sandwiches. The shop charged $235 for all the ham sandwiches,
$225 for all the turkey sandwiches, and $217.30 for all the meatball sandwiches. How much
does each sandwich cost?

_____

Problem Solving Strategies 5, SV 0516-2

Unit 5 Review

Strategies

- Choose an Operation
- Identify Substeps
- Guess and Check
- Work Backward
- Use Estimation
- Make a Table

Show What You Know!

Solve each problem. Identify the strategy you used.

1. Georgie, Gina, and Gillian are triplets. Their parents gave them a total of 1 dozen roses after they performed in the school play. If all the girls got the same number of roses, how many flowers did each girl get? (Remember: 1 dozen = 12)

_____

2. Shiro is 12. He is 4 years younger than Suki. Chen is half Shiro's age, and Min is half Suki's age. How old are Suki, Chen, and Min?

_____

3. Claire will walk every day for 6 days. She wants to walk the same number of miles each day for a total of 30 miles. How many miles should she walk each day?

_____

4. Vince went to a sale. He bought some things for his dog. He spent $4.00 on 4 leashes, $6.00 on 24 dog treats, and $2.00 on 4 toys. How much did he spend on each item he bought?

_____

_____

_____

5. The number of shelves on each bookcase is a 1-digit number. The number of shelves per bookcase is 2 times the number of bookcases. There are 32 shelves total. What is the number of bookcases?

_____

What is the number of shelves per bookcase?

_____

Unit 5 Review, page 2

Show What You Know!

Solve each problem. Identify the strategy you used.

1. The number of students in a classroom is a 2-digit number. The number of students sitting in each row is a 1-digit number. The number of rows is 2 less than the number of students in each row. The number of students divided by the number of rows is 7. What is the number of students in the classroom?

_____

2. A train traveled 6,431 miles in 12 trips. If the train traveled to the same location each time, about how many miles did it travel on each trip?

_____

3. A uniform factory makes 125 white shirts, 250 blue shirts, and 100 green shirts. The white shirts will be divided equally among 5 District A schools. The blue shirts will be divided equally among 10 District B schools. The green shirts will be equally divided among 4 District C schools. How many shirts will each school get? Make a table to help you solve the problem.

_____

Extension

Find out how many fifth grade students there are in your school. Then find out how many fifth grade classrooms there are. About how many students are in each fifth grade class?

Name _____ Date _____

FLEX YOUR MATH MUSCLES

1

Flex is traveling across a desert without roads and asks some of his friends to help. He will have to hike for 6 days to reach the other side. Each person, including Flex, can carry 4 days' supply of food and water. How many friends will have to go with him, and how will they get him across the desert?

_____

_____

2

Flex has 2 books standing side by side on a shelf. A bookworm ate its way through the books, starting at page 1 of Volume 1. It had gotten to the last page of Volume 2 when Flex discovered the damage and stepped on the bookworm. Each book cover was $\frac{1}{8}$ of an inch thick. The pages of the books without the covers were 2 inches thick. How far had the bookworm traveled?

_____

3

Do you collect coins? Do you know that 1966 pennies are worth almost $20? Do you know why?

_____

_____

Problem Solving Strategies 5, SV 0516-2

Name _____ Date _____

FRACTION ZONE

Strategy: Use a Drawing

Fractions name equal parts of a whole or equal parts of a group. If a pizza is cut into 4 equal slices, each slice is $\frac{1}{4}$, or one-fourth, of the whole pizza. Use a drawing to see the parts.

numerator ——→ $\dfrac{1}{4}$ ←—— one shaded part

denominator ——→ $\phantom{\dfrac{1}{4}}$ ←—— four parts in all

If the pizza is cut into 5 pieces and 2 of them are eaten, then $\frac{2}{5}$, or two-fifths, of the pizza has been eaten.

numerator ——→ $\dfrac{2}{5}$ ←—— two shaded parts

denominator ——→ $\phantom{\dfrac{2}{5}}$ ←—— five parts in all

STEP 1 ▷ Read the problem.
Write the fraction and the word name for the part that is shaded.

STEP 2 ▷ Identify the facts.
The rectangle has 8 equal parts.
3 of the 8 equal parts are shaded.

STEP 3 ▷ Use the drawing. Solve the problem.
$\frac{3}{8}$, or three-eighths, of the rectangle is shaded.

Try It!   Use the drawings to write fractions for the shaded parts.

1. _____

3. _____

2. _____

4. _____

Problem Solving Strategies 5, SV 0516-2

Name _____ Date _____

EQUIVALENT FRACTIONS

Strategy: Use a Drawing

Equivalent fractions are different names for the same amount. Compare the shaded parts of the same size squares. The shaded part of one square is equal to the shaded part of the other square.

$\frac{1}{2}$ of the square is shaded.

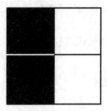

$\frac{2}{4}$ of the square is shaded.

$\frac{1}{2}$ and $\frac{2}{4}$ are equivalent fractions.

STEP 1 **Read the problem.**
How many eighths are equal to $\frac{3}{4}$ of a square?

STEP 2 **Identify what the problem asks.**
Write the equivalent number of eighths for three-fourths.

STEP 3 **Solve the problem.**
Draw a square. Shade $\frac{3}{4}$. Make eighths.
Note how many are shaded.

$\frac{3}{4} = \frac{6}{8}$

Try It! Use or make drawings to solve these problems.

1. Use the squares shown above. How many eighths are in $\frac{1}{2}$?

_____

2. How many eighths are in $\frac{2}{4}$?

_____

3. Write two equivalent fractions for the shaded part of this figure.

_____

_____

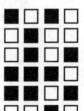

Unit 6, Fractions
Problem Solving Strategies 5, SV 0516-2

SLIDING AWAY

Strategy: Choose an Operation

When you do not know whether to add or subtract, look at the action. Joining parts or groups usually means addition. Separating, taking away, or comparing parts or groups usually means subtraction.

STEP 1 **Read the problem.**

At the swim club meeting, $\frac{7}{8}$ of the members showed up. They all practiced swimming. Then $\frac{3}{8}$ of the members practiced diving. What part of the club practiced swimming but did not practice diving?

STEP 2 **Identify what the problem asks. Choose an operation.**

The problem asks you to separate the part that practiced diving from the part that practiced swimming. You should subtract.

STEP 3 **Subtract. Solve the problem.**

$\frac{7}{8} - \frac{3}{8} = \frac{4}{8}$

$\frac{4}{8}$, or $\frac{1}{2}$, of the membership practiced swimming but did not practice diving.

Try It! Choose the operation. Then solve the problems.

1. During an ice skating class, $\frac{5}{6}$ of the class did spins and $\frac{2}{6}$ of the class fell. What part of the skating class did spins without falling?

_____

2. At the ski club's first meeting, $\frac{5}{8}$ of those who promised to attend did show up on time. Another $\frac{1}{8}$ showed up late. What part of those who promised to attend really did?

_____

Name _____ Date _____

SIMPLY SO.....

Strategy: Write a Number Sentence

Sometimes you need to use a fraction in simplest terms as the answer. Simplest terms means that the numerator and the denominator have no common factor other than 1. For example, $\frac{6}{8}$ is not in simplest terms, because both 6 and 8 can be divided by 2. $\frac{3}{4}$ is in simplest terms. Write number sentences to reduce fractions to simplest, or lowest, terms.

$$\frac{6}{8} \div \frac{2}{2} = \frac{6 \div 2}{8 \div 2} = \frac{3}{4}$$

STEP 1 **Read the problem.**
Jim ate $\frac{1}{6}$ of the pan pizza. Jenny ate $\frac{1}{6}$ of the pan pizza. What part of the whole pizza did they eat? Express your answer in simplest terms.

STEP 2 **Identify what the problem asks.**
The problem asks what fraction in simplest terms equals $\frac{1}{6} + \frac{1}{6}$.

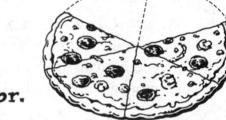

STEP 3 **Identify the common factor.**
Step 1: $\frac{1}{6} + \frac{1}{6} = \frac{2}{6}$
Step 2: 2 is the common factor of 2 and 6.

STEP 4 **Write a number sentence to solve the problem.**
$\frac{2}{6} \div \frac{2}{2} = \frac{2 \div 2}{6 \div 2} = \frac{1}{3}$
Jim and Jenny ate $\frac{1}{3}$ of the pizza.

Try It! Write a number sentence to solve each problem. Express answers in simplest terms.

1. Ginger cut the gingerbread into 10 equal pieces. She gave 2 to her mother and 3 to her father. What part of the whole gingerbread did she give away?

_____

2. Angela cut the angel food cake into 16 equal pieces. She gave 3 pieces to her friends and 1 to herself. What part of the whole cake did she give away?

_____

Problem Solving Strategies 5, SV 0516-2

Name _____ Date _____

IT'S MARKING TIME

Strategy: Make a Drawing

To add or subtract fractions, make sure the fractions have the same denominator. If they do not, rename one or both of the fractions. Make a drawing to help you.

STEP 1 ▷ **Read the problem.**

Kerry uses $\frac{5}{12}$ of her 12 markers. Kevin uses $\frac{1}{3}$ of Kerry's markers. Altogether, what part of the group of markers did Kerry and Kevin use?

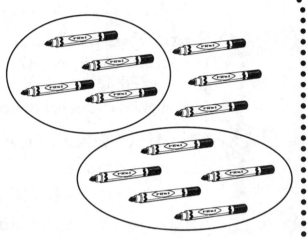

STEP 2 ▷ **Identify what the problem asks.**

The problem asks what fraction equals $\frac{5}{12} + \frac{1}{3}$.

STEP 3 ▷ **Change one or both fractions to have a common denominator.**

Step 1: Find the least common multiple of the denominators.

Multiples of 3: 3, 6, 9, 12, 15...
Multiples of 12: 12, 24, 36, 48...
The least common multiple is 12.

Step 2: Change the fractions to the least common multiple.

$\frac{1}{3} \times \frac{4}{4} = \frac{1 \times 4}{3 \times 4} = \frac{4}{12}$

STEP 4 ▷ **Add. Solve the problem.**

$\frac{5}{12} + \frac{1}{3} = \frac{5}{12} + \frac{4}{12} = \frac{9}{12}$ $\frac{9}{12}$, or $\frac{3}{4}$, of the markers were used.

Try It! Make a drawing and find equivalent fractions to solve this problem.

1. A street crew must mark new stripes on 12 streets. On Monday, they mark $\frac{1}{4}$ of the 12 streets. On Tuesday, they mark $\frac{2}{3}$ of the 12 streets. What part of the 12 streets in all have been marked?

_____

Problem Solving Strategies 5, SV 0516-2

SCHOOL DAZE

Strategy: Choose an Operation

When you do not know whether to add or subtract, look at the action. Joining parts or groups usually means addition. Separating, taking away, or comparing parts or groups usually means subtraction.

STEP 1 **Read the problem.**

The physical education teacher had $\frac{1}{6}$ of his middle school classes climb a rope and $\frac{2}{3}$ of his elementary school classes climb a ladder. Altogether, what fraction of his classes did climbing activities?

STEP 2 **Identify what the problem asks. Choose an operation.**

The problem asks for the parts altogether. *Altogether* signals addition. $\frac{1}{6} + \frac{2}{3}$

STEP 3 **Change the fractions to the least common denominator.**

Step 1: Multiples of 6: 6, 12, 18, 24...
　　　　　Multiples of 3: 3, 6, 9, 12, 15...
　　　　　The least common denominator is 6.

Step 2: Write the fractions with the least common denominator.
　　　　　$\frac{1}{6} = \frac{1}{6}$ 　　 $\frac{2}{3} = \frac{4}{6}$

STEP 4 **Add. Solve the problem.**

Add the fractions. $\frac{1}{6} + \frac{4}{6} = \frac{5}{6}$
$\frac{5}{6}$ of the classes did climbing activities.

Try It! Choose the operation. Then solve the problems.

1. It took the fourth grade class $\frac{11}{12}$ of an hour to finish their project. It took the fifth grade class $\frac{1}{4}$ of an hour to finish their project. How much longer did it take the fourth grade class?

_____

How many minutes is that?

2. After school, Toni did $\frac{3}{10}$ of her math homework. After dinner, she did $\frac{2}{5}$ more. How much did she do in all?

_____

How much more does she have to do?

_____

Name _____ Date _____

IMPROPER FRACTIONS

Strategy: Use a Drawing

An improper fraction is a fraction with a numerator equal to or greater than its denominator. The amount named by an improper fraction can also be named by a whole number or a mixed number. Use drawings to help you.

improper fraction ———→ $\frac{5}{5} = 1$ ←——— whole number

improper fraction ———→ $\frac{7}{5} = 1\frac{2}{5}$ ←——— mixed number

STEP 1 **Read the problem.**
Write the improper fraction and the mixed number for the shaded parts.

STEP 2 **Identify what you know.**
There are 3 squares. Each has 2 halves. 5 halves are shaded.

STEP 3 **Use the drawing. Solve the problem.**
The improper fraction is $\frac{5}{2}$.
The mixed number is $2\frac{1}{2}$.

Try It! Use drawings to help you solve the problems.

1. Write the improper fraction and the mixed number for the shaded parts.

   _____ _____

2. Draw pictures to show these improper fractions. Then write a mixed number for each.

   $\frac{3}{2} =$ _____

   $\frac{5}{4} =$ _____

   $\frac{5}{3} =$ _____

Unit 6, Fractions
Problem Solving Strategies 5, SV 0516-2

Unit 6 Review

Strategies
- Use a Drawing
- Choose an Operation
- Write a Number Sentence
- Make a Drawing

Show What You Know!

Solve each problem. Identify the strategy you used.

---

1. Write two equivalent fractions for the shaded part of this figure.

_____

2. Use the drawing to write a fraction for the shaded part.

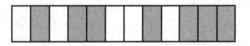

_____

3. Jena did $\frac{2}{3}$ of her homework Saturday morning and $\frac{1}{6}$ of her homework that afternoon. How much homework did Jenna have left to do on Sunday?

_____

4. Tom and Andrew have 15 video games. They like to play different games. Tom likes to play $\frac{1}{3}$ of the games. Andrew likes to play $\frac{7}{15}$ of the games. Altogether, what part of the games do Tom and Andrew like to play? Make a drawing and find equivalent fractions to solve this problem.

_____

5. Lisa ate $\frac{2}{8}$ of a pizza and her brother ate $\frac{3}{8}$ of the pizza. How much of the pizza did Lisa and her brother eat?

_____

Unit 6 Review, page 2

Show What You Know!

Solve each problem. Identify the strategy you used.

1. Dana bought a set of 6 mystery books. She read 2 the first week and 2 the second week. What part of the set of mystery books did Dana read? Express the answer in simplest terms.

_____

2. At a book club meeting $\frac{5}{6}$ of the members showed up. That evening $\frac{2}{6}$ of the club gave a book report. What part of the club came to the meeting but did not give a book report?

_____

3. Mrs. Washington baked 20 cupcakes for her students. She put chocolate icing on $\frac{8}{20}$ of the cupcakes and vanilla icing on $\frac{1}{4}$ of the cupcakes. She put strawberry icing on the rest of the cupcakes. What part of the cupcakes had strawberry icing? Make a drawing and find equivalent fractions to solve this problem.

_____

4. Use the drawing to write a fraction for the shaded part.

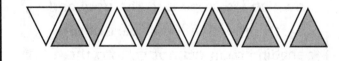

_____

Extension

Count the number of students in your class. Then take a separate count of the number of boys and the number of girls. Tell what fraction of students in your class are boys. Tell what fraction of students in your class are girls.

Name _____ Date _____

FLEX YOUR MATH MUSCLES

Flex has had fun problem solving with fractions. He wants to review not only the parts, but also the whole!

1

What part of a year is 5 months?

_____

2

What part of a dollar is 7 dimes?

_____

3

At the zoo, $\frac{7}{10}$ of the penguins slid down an ice slope into the pool and $\frac{1}{10}$ just jumped in. What part of the penguin group did not go into the pool at all?

_____

4

At the preschool playground, $\frac{9}{15}$ of the children used only the swings, and $\frac{3}{15}$ of the children used only the slide. The rest of the children used both. What part of the group used both the swings and slide?

_____

5

The Jefferson School Hiking Club met for a hike on Saturday. They walked $\frac{3}{10}$ of a mile in the morning and another $\frac{7}{10}$ of a mile in the afternoon. How much farther did they walk in the afternoon?

_____

DIFFERENT YET ALIKE

Strategy: Find Equivalent Fractions

To add or subtract fractions with different denominators, change one or both fractions to equivalent fractions. To do this, find the least common multiple of the denominators.

STEP 1 ▷ Read the problem.

A brother and sister living on a farm were doing their chores. John filled his bucket $\frac{1}{2}$ full with water. Joan filled her bucket $\frac{1}{4}$ full. Together, how much did they fill the buckets?

STEP 2 ▷ Identify the facts.

One bucket is $\frac{1}{2}$ filled, the other is $\frac{1}{4}$ filled.

STEP 3 ▷ Change one or both fractions to the least common denominator.

Step 1: List the multiples of each number. Do not use zero.
Multiples of 2: 2, 4, 6, 8, 10, and so forth
Multiples of 4: 4, 8, 12, 16, 20, and so forth

Step 2: Identify the least common multiple: 4
Change both denominators to 4. $\frac{1}{2} \times \frac{2}{2} = \frac{2}{4}$ $\frac{1}{4} = \frac{1}{4}$

STEP 4 ▷ Solve the problem.

Add the two fractions. $\frac{2}{4} + \frac{1}{4} = \frac{3}{4}$
They filled $\frac{3}{4}$ of the buckets.

Try It! Find the least common multiples of the denominators. Then solve the problems.

1. Joan filled her bucket to the top. She then poured $\frac{1}{3}$ of her bucket into John's bucket. How much did she have left?

_____

2. John had his bucket $\frac{1}{2}$ full after Joan poured the water into his bucket. How full was his bucket before Joan added water from her bucket?

_____

DIFFERENT YET ALIKE, part 2

Strategy: Choose an Operation

When you do not know whether to add or subtract, look at the action. Joining parts or groups usually means addition. Separating, taking away, or comparing parts or groups usually means subtraction.

STEP 1 ▶ **Read the problem.**

Two eggshells broke into 9 pieces each. Sam found $\frac{1}{6}$ of the pieces. His friend found $\frac{1}{9}$ of the pieces. Together what part of the eggshell pieces did they find?

STEP 2 ▶ **Identify what the problem asks. Choose an operation.**

The problem asks how much of the eggshell pieces they found together. The word *together* signals addition. You should add.

STEP 3 ▶ **Solve the problem.**

Step 1: **A.** Find the least common multiple.
   B. Multiples of 6: 6, 12, 18. Multiples of 9: 9, 18, 27.
   C. The least common multiple is 18.

Step 2: **A.** Change the fractions into equivalent fractions.
   B. $\frac{1}{6} = \frac{3}{18}$ $\frac{1}{9} = \frac{2}{18}$ $\frac{3}{18} + \frac{2}{18} = \frac{5}{18}$
   C. Sam and his friend found $\frac{5}{18}$ of the eggshell pieces.

Try It! Choose the operation. Then solve the problems.

1. Sam and his friend used the egg to bake a pie. Sam ate $\frac{1}{6}$ of the pie. His friend ate $\frac{1}{4}$. Altogether how much of the pie did they eat?

   _____

2. How much more or less than $\frac{1}{2}$ of the pie was left?

   _____

Name _____ Date _____

DESSERT, ANYONE?

Strategy: Choose an Operation

To add or subtract mixed numbers with different denominators, write the fractions with the same denominators. Add or subtract the fractions. Then add or subtract the whole numbers. Simplify the answer.

 Read the problem.
Sherry bought $2\frac{1}{2}$ apple pies and $3\frac{1}{4}$ blueberry pies. How many pies did she buy?

 Identify what the problem asks. Choose an operation.
The problem asks, "How many pies did Sherry buy altogether?" The word *altogether* signals addition.

STEP 3 **Change one or both fractions to have a common denominator.**
Step 1: List the multiples of each denominator:
Multiples of 2: 2, 4, 6, 8.
Multiples of 4: 4, 8, 12, 16.
Choose the least common multiple: 4.
Step 2: Change the fractions into equivalent fractions:
$\frac{1}{2} = \frac{2}{4}$ $\frac{1}{4} = \frac{1}{4}$

 Add. Solve the problem.
Write the mixed numbers with like denominators. Add the fractions.
Then add the whole numbers. $2\frac{2}{4} + 3\frac{1}{4} = 5\frac{3}{4}$
Sherry bought $5\frac{3}{4}$ pies.

Try It!   Choose an operation. Find the least common denominator. Solve the problems.

1. Sherry had $2\frac{1}{2}$ apple pies. She gave away $\frac{1}{3}$ of one of the pies. How much did she have left?

   _____

2. The next day, Sherry bought $2\frac{1}{3}$ apple pies, $3\frac{1}{2}$ blueberry pies, and $4\frac{1}{6}$ lemon pies. Altogether how many pies did she buy?

   _____

Name _____   Date _____

DESSERT, ANYONE? part 2

Strategy: Choose an Operation

Sometimes a problem does not tell you to add or subtract. Decide what the problem is asking you to do. Change the mixed numbers with different denominators into mixed numbers with equivalent fractions. Then solve the problem.

STEP 1 **Read the problem.**
Little Jack Horner ate $2\frac{1}{4}$ plum puddings and $4\frac{3}{5}$ cinnamon buns. How many desserts did he eat altogether?

STEP 2 **Identify the facts.**
Jack ate $2\frac{1}{4}$ puddings and $4\frac{3}{5}$ buns.

STEP 3 **Choose an operation.**
The problem asks, "How many desserts did he eat altogether?" The word *altogether* signals addition.

Step 1: Find the least common multiples of the denominators.
Multiples of 4: 4, 8, 12, 16, 20, and so on.
Multiples of 5: 5, 10, 15, 20, and so on.
The least common multiple is 20.

Step 2: Change the fractions into equivalent fractions with the least common denominator. $\frac{1}{4} = \frac{5}{20}$ $\frac{3}{5} = \frac{12}{20}$

STEP 4 **Add. Solve the problem.**
Add the fractions. $\frac{5}{20} + \frac{12}{20} = \frac{17}{20}$ Add the whole numbers. $2 + 4 = 6$
Then add the whole numbers and fractions. Jack ate $6\frac{17}{20}$ desserts.

Try It! Choose an operation. Find equivalent fractions to solve the problems.

1. Jack ate $1\frac{1}{4}$ mince pies and $1\frac{2}{5}$ apple pies. How much pie did he eat altogether?

_____

2. The next day, Mother baked $2\frac{1}{2}$ pies. She gave the neighbor $1\frac{1}{3}$ pies. How much pie did she have left?

_____

72
Unit 7, Fractions and Mixed Numbers
Problem Solving Strategies 5, SV 0516-2

Name _____ Date _____

HAVE YOU ANY WOOL?

Strategy: Change Whole Numbers to Fractions

Sometimes you will subtract a fraction from a whole number. To do this, change the whole number to a mixed number with a like denominator. Subtract the fractions, then subtract the whole numbers.

STEP 1 ▷ Read the problem.
After shearing sheep, Juan had 6 bags of wool. He sold $4\frac{2}{3}$ bags of wool. How many bags of wool were left?

STEP 2 ▷ Identify the facts.
Fact 1: Juan had 6 bags of wool.
Fact 2: He sold $4\frac{2}{3}$ bags.

STEP 3 ▷ Identify what the problem asks.
The problem asks, "How many bags were left?"

STEP 4 ▷ Change the whole number to a mixed number with a like denominator.
$6 = 5 + \frac{3}{3}$

STEP 5 ▷ Subtract. Solve the problem.
Subtract the fractions. Then subtract the whole numbers.
$5\frac{3}{3} - 4\frac{2}{3} = 1\frac{1}{3}$ bags of wool are left.

 Try It! Change the whole numbers to mixed numbers with a like denominator to solve these problems.

1. Juan had 12 more bags of wool. He took $7\frac{5}{8}$ bags to market. How many bags did he keep?

_____

2. Silencia made 4 dozen candles. She sold $1\frac{3}{4}$ dozen. How many dozen did she keep?

_____

Name _____   Date _____

HAVE YOU ANY WOOL? part 2

Strategy: Identify Extra or Missing Information

Some problems give too many facts. Other problems don't give enough facts. Read the problem carefully. If there are too many facts, cross out the extra facts. If there are not enough facts, decide what you need to know. Then solve the problem.

 Read the problem.

The cook in a small preschool cooked $10\frac{1}{2}$ pots of soup. She also cooked $6\frac{3}{4}$ pots of oatmeal. She had to feed 26 children. How many pots of food did she cook?

 Identify what the problem asks.

The problem asks how many pots of food she cooked.

STEP 3 **Identify the facts and any extra or missing facts.**

Facts: $10\frac{1}{2}$ pots of soup and $6\frac{3}{4}$ pots of oatmeal
Extra fact: She had 26 children to feed.

STEP 4 **Add. Solve the problem.**

Step 1: Change the fractions into equivalent fractions.
$$10\frac{1}{2} = 10\frac{4}{8} \qquad 6\frac{3}{4} = 6\frac{6}{8}$$
Step 2: Add the fractions. $\qquad \frac{4}{8} + \frac{6}{8} = \frac{10}{8} = 1\frac{2}{8}$
Step 3: Add the whole numbers. $\quad 10 + 6 = 16$
Step 4: Simplify the answer. $\quad 16 + 1\frac{2}{8} = 17\frac{2}{8}$ or $17\frac{1}{4}$

Try It!

Cross out extra facts. If facts are missing, write the facts. Then solve the problems.

1. Grandmother Hubbard baked for the twins who are 11 years old. They ate $2\frac{3}{4}$ chocolate cakes and $3\frac{1}{8}$ angel food cakes. How many cakes did they eat?

_____

2. Her neighbor blew up 5 balloons and brought $2\frac{5}{6}$ dozen cupcakes. The children ate $1\frac{1}{2}$ dozen cupcakes. How many were left?

_____

Unit 7, Fractions and Mixed Numbers
Problem Solving Strategies 5, SV 0516-2

REVIEW WITH RHYMES

Strategy: Choose an Operation

Try It! Choose an operation. Solve the problems.

1. Jack and Jill filled their buckets. On the way down the hill, Jack spilled $\frac{1}{6}$ of his bucket. Jill spilled $\frac{1}{4}$ of hers. How much water did they spill together?

_____

2. In Mary Contrary's garden, $\frac{2}{3}$ of the flowers are silver bells or daisies. If $\frac{1}{2}$ of her flowers are daisies, what part of her flowers are silver bells?

_____

3. The Queen of Hearts made 5 dozen tarts. She gave away $2\frac{1}{4}$ dozen. How many dozen did she keep?

_____

4. The King of Hearts found 6 tarts and ate $3\frac{1}{3}$. How many were left?

_____

5. The twins had $4\frac{2}{5}$ bags of coins. They lost $2\frac{1}{3}$ bags of coins. How many bags did they have left?

_____

6. Little Bo Peep looked for her sheep for $3\frac{1}{4}$ hours on Monday and $6\frac{1}{2}$ hours on Tuesday. How many hours did she look in all?

_____

7. Jack was nimble and jumped $3\frac{3}{4}$ feet over the candlestick. Peter could only jump $1\frac{1}{3}$ feet. How much higher was Jack's jump than Peter's?

_____

8. You rowed the boat gently down the stream for $8\frac{1}{6}$ miles in the morning. After lunch, you rowed $6\frac{2}{3}$ miles. How far did you row the boat altogether?

_____

Unit 7 Review

Show What You Know!

Solve each problem. Identify the strategy you used.

---

1. Naomi bought a necklace that was on sale for $\frac{1}{3}$ off. When she got to the cash register, the clerk told her that the store was having a special with all items being another $\frac{1}{4}$ off. Altogether, what fraction did Naomi get to take off the price of the necklace?

_____

2. Rusty bought several pizzas for a party. He ordered $1\frac{1}{2}$ pepperoni, $2\frac{1}{4}$ sausage, $1\frac{1}{4}$ cheese, $1\frac{1}{3}$ vegetables with mushrooms, and $\frac{2}{3}$ vegetables without mushrooms. How many pizzas did he buy altogether?

_____

3. Kyle got a new photo album that was on sale for $\frac{1}{2}$ price. He filled $\frac{2}{3}$ of the pages with pictures of his birthday party and $\frac{1}{4}$ of the pages with pictures of his vacation. What part of the photo album does not have any pictures yet?

_____

4. Sonya worked on her math homework for $\frac{1}{2}$ hour and her science homework for $\frac{1}{3}$ hour. How much time did Sonya spend on her homework altogether?

_____

5. The shelf that Eduardo is making requires $\frac{7}{8}$ foot of lumber. Eduardo has $\frac{1}{2}$ foot of lumber. How much more lumber does he need?

_____

Name _____ Date _____

Unit 7 Review, page 2

Show What You Know!

Solve each problem. Identify the strategy you used.

1. Flynn worked at a bike shop. He painted $\frac{1}{3}$ of the bikes red and $\frac{1}{6}$ red with a white stripe. What part of the bikes had some red on them?

_____

2. Bert bought $\frac{3}{8}$ pound of American cheese and $\frac{1}{4}$ pound of Swiss cheese. How much cheese did Bert buy altogether?

_____

3. Cameron had 7 bags to fill with leaves that she raked from her yard. She has already filled $3\frac{1}{4}$ bags. How many bags does she still need to fill?

_____

4. Minerva and her grandmother spent $1\frac{1}{2}$ hours baking cookies. They gave $1\frac{1}{4}$ dozen cookies to their neighbors that live on one side and $1\frac{1}{4}$ dozen cookies to their neighbors that live on the other side. How many dozen cookies did they give to their neighbors?

_____

5. Roger collected baseball cards. He traded $\frac{1}{6}$ of his cards with Jake and some of his cards with Sue. What part of his cards did Roger trade altogether?

_____

Extension

Use a map or a car odometer to find out how far it is from your home to your school. Write that distance using a fraction or mixed number. Figure out how many miles you travel to go to school in 1 day and 1 week. Remember that you usually only go to school on weekdays and that you travel to and from school each day.

Name _____ Date _____

FLEX YOUR MATH MUSCLES

1

Flex was riding his motorscooter when he ran out of gas. A friendly motorist stopped to help. Flex's gas tank held exactly 2 gallons. The motorist had a 5-gallon can and an 8-gallon can. How did Flex use these cans to measure 2 gallons exactly?

_____

_____

_____

_____

_____

_____

2

Which would you rather have: a bag with 4 pounds of $10 gold coins or a bag with 2 pounds of $20 gold coins? Which bag is worth more? (Hint: the number of coins in each bag is not important.)

_____

_____

_____

_____

_____

_____

3

Meile has to paint a wall of her house. She is painting while standing on the middle rung of a ladder. She paints in a strange way. She goes up 5 rungs, down 7 rungs, up 4 rungs, and then up 9 more rungs to reach the top rung. How many rungs are there on the ladder?

_____

Unit 7, Fractions and Mixed Numbers
Problem Solving Strategies 5, SV 0516-2

Name _____ Date _____

FORMULAS ARE FRIENDS

Strategy: Use a Formula

The facts in a problem may be expressed in a formula. Use the formula with the facts to solve the problem.

Area of a rectangle = length × width
$A = L \times W$
Area is the number of square units inside a figure.
In a rectangle that is 3 × 2, the area is 6 square units.

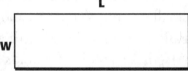

Area of a square = one side × itself
$A = S \times S$
In a square that is 4 × 4, the area is 16 square units.

STEP 1 **Read the problem.**
Chong's bedroom is 10 feet long and 12 feet wide. What is the area?

STEP 2 **Use the formula.**
Use the formula for the area of a rectangle. $A = L \times W$
Use the numbers in the formula. A = 10 feet × 12 feet

STEP 3 **Multiply. Solve the problem.**
A = 120 square feet. The area of the bedroom is 120 square feet.

Try It! Use the formula to solve each problem. Copy the formula and use the numbers in the formula.

1. Mr. George is carpeting his living room. It is 15 feet long and 12 feet wide. Find the area of the room.

_____

2. Mrs. George wants a square rug for the living room. One side is 5 feet. How much area will it cover?

_____

3. Jan is putting crepe paper on a door that measures 6 feet high and 3 feet wide. How many square feet of crepe paper will she need?

_____

Name _____ Date _____

POURING IT ON!

Strategy: Use Estimation

Capacity is measured in cups, pints, quarts, and gallons. The chart shows the relationship of these units. The smallest unit is the cup, and the largest unit is the gallon. A milk carton with a school lunch holds 1 cup. A sports water bottle holds about 1 quart. A small sink holds about 1 gallon.

1 pint (pt)	= **2 cups (c)**
1 quart (qt)	= **2 pt or 4 c**
1 gallon (g)	= **4 qt or 8 pt or 16 c**

 STEP 1 > **Define the object as small, medium, or large.**
a mug of hot chocolate   small

 STEP 2 > **Identify the appropriate unit.**
The capacity of small objects is measured in cups.

STEP 3 > **Estimate the capacity.**
Solve the problem.
a mug of hot chocolate   ____ cup

Try It! Estimate the capacity and identify the appropriate unit. Use *cup, pint, quart,* or *gallon.*

1. a container of whipping cream _____

2. a science beaker _____

3. a swimming pool _____

4. an aquarium _____

5. a bowl of soup _____

6. a pan _____

7. a bucket _____

8. a bottle of soda _____

Problem Solving Strategies 5, SV 0516-2

CUPS, PINTS, QUARTS, AND GALLONS

Strategy: Choose an Operation

To measure capacity or volume, use cups, pints, quarts, and gallons. To change from one unit to another, multiply or divide. To change from larger units to smaller ones, multiply. To change from smaller units to larger ones, divide.

> **1 pint = 2 cups**
> **1 quart = 2 pints or 4 cups**
> **1 gallon = 4 quarts or 8 pints or 16 cups**

Example 1:

3 quarts = ? pints
To change quarts to pints, multiply.
1 quart = 2 pints
$3 \times 2 = 6$
3 quarts = 6 pints

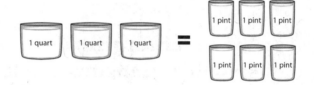

Example 2:

16 pints = ? gallons
To change pints to gallons, divide.
8 pints = 1 gallon
$16 \div 8 = 2$
16 pints = 2 gallons

Try It! Use the chart. Choose an operation. Solve the problems.

1. 8 cups = _____ quarts

2. 8 cups = _____ pints

3. 6 pints = _____ quarts

4. 4 gallons = _____ quarts

5. 4 gallons = _____ pints

6. 20 quarts = _____ gallons

Name _____ Date _____

INCHES, FEET, AND YARDS

Strategy: Choose an Operation

To measure length, use inches, feet, and yards. To change from one unit to another, multiply or divide. When changing from a larger unit to a smaller unit, multiply. When changing from a smaller unit to a larger unit, divide.

12 inches = 1 foot	36 inches = 1 yard	3 feet = 1 yard

STEP 1 **Read the problem.**
A bowling lane is about 3 feet wide. How many inches wide is it?

STEP 2 **Use the chart.**
1 foot = 12 inches

STEP 3 **When changing from a larger measure to a smaller measure, multiply. Solve the problem.**
3 × 12 = 36
3 feet = 36 inches

Try It! Choose the operation. Write a number sentence. Solve the problems.

1. Sonia used 8 yards of canvas for her pup tent. How many feet did she use?

_____

2. Carol bought 5 yards of wool. How many inches is this?

_____

3. A football field is 3,600 inches long. How many yards is it?

_____

4. A bowling lane is about 60 feet long. How many yards is it?

_____

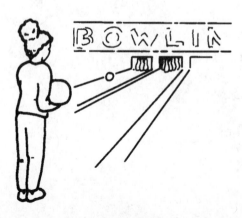

Problem Solving Strategies 5, SV 0516-2

Name _____ Date _____

OUNCES, POUNDS, AND TONS

Strategy: Choose an Operation

To measure weight, use ounces, pounds, and tons. To change from one unit to another, multiply or divide.

1 pound (1 lb) = 16 ounces (oz)
1 ton (T) = 2,000 pounds (lb)

To change pounds to a smaller unit such as ounces, multiply. To find how many ounces are in 3 pounds, multiply by 3.

1 lb = 16 oz
3 × 16 = 48
3 lb = 48 oz

To change pounds to a larger unit such as tons, divide. To find how many tons are in 4,000 pounds, divide by 2,000.

2,000 lb = 1 T
4,000 ÷ 2,000 = 2
4,000 lb = 2 T

STEP 1 **Read the problem.**
Your dog weighs 14 pounds. How many ounces does your dog weigh?

STEP 2 **Identify what the problem asks.**
The problem asks how many ounces are in 14 pounds.

STEP 3 **To find the number of ounces, change from a larger measure to a smaller measure by multiplying.**

STEP 4 **Multiply. Solve the problem.**
14 pounds = ? ounces
1 pound = 16 ounces
16 × 14 = 224
14 pounds = 224 ounces

Name _____ Date _____

OUNCES, POUNDS, AND TONS, part 2

Strategy: Use a Chart

Try It! To change the unit of measure, use the chart. Choose an operation. Solve the problems.

1 pound (lb)	=	16 ounces (oz)
1 ton (T)	=	2,000 pounds

1. You buy dog food that weighs 160 ounces. How many pounds are in the bag?

   _____

2. The neighbor's cat eats 8 ounces of food each day. How many pounds of food will the cat eat in 8 days?

   _____

3. The zoo elephant weighs about 3 tons. How many pounds is this?

   _____

4. The orchard produced 14,000 pounds of grapes. How many tons is this?

   _____

5. The neighbor's cat weighs 10 pounds. How many ounces is this?

   _____

6. You catch a fish that weighs 32 ounces. How many pounds is this?

   _____

7. The concrete used for a driveway weighs 10,000 pounds. How many tons is this?

   _____

8. Ignacio weighed 8 pounds when he was born. How many ounces did he weigh?

   _____

Problem Solving Strategies 5, SV 0516-2

Name _____ Date _____

A LONG WAY AROUND

Strategy: Use a Formula

The facts in a problem may be expressed in a formula. Use the formula with the facts to solve the problem.

Perimeter is the distance around a figure.
The perimeter of a rectangle is found by using this formula:

$$\text{Perimeter} = 2 \times \text{length} + 2 \times \text{width}$$
$$\text{or}$$
$$P = 2L + 2W$$

 STEP 1 **Read the problem.**
The table in the science lab is 6 feet by 3 feet. What is the perimeter?

STEP 2 **Use the formula.**
$P = 2L + 2W$
$P = 2(6) + 2(3)$
$P = 12 + 6$
$P = 18$

STEP 3 **Solve the problem.**
$P = 18$
The perimeter of the table is 18 ft.

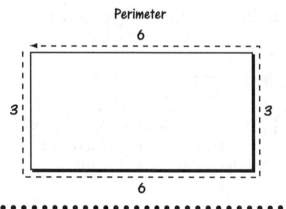

Try It! Use the formula to solve each problem.

1. A classroom measures 50 ft by 30 ft. To walk around the outer edge, how far is it? Find the perimeter.

_____

2. The largest banner in the world announced the arrival of the Ringling Bros. Barnum and Bailey Circus in Dallas, Texas. The banner was 320 ft by 18 ft. What was its perimeter?

_____

3. A school is on a lot that is 250 yd by 150 yd. To walk around the outer edge, how far is it?

_____

4. The largest poster in the world was made in Japan for the Obihiro festival. It measured 328 ft by 328 ft. If a wooden frame was placed around it, how many feet of wood was needed?

_____

Name _____ Date _____

Unit 8 Review

Strategies
- Use a Formula
- Use Estimation
- Choose an Operation
- Use a Chart

Show What You Know!

Solve each problem. Identify the strategy you used.

1. How many pints are in 3 gallons? (Hint: 1 gallon = 8 pints)

_____

2. Veronica wanted to hang wallpaper on a wall that measured 12 feet by 8 feet. What is the area of the wall?

_____

3. Veronica decided to put a border on her 12 foot by 8 foot wall. What is the perimeter of the wall?

_____

4. What unit would you use to measure the capacity of a bathtub?

_____

5. To grow a vegetable garden, Leticia cleared a piece of land that measured 6 feet by 8 feet. What was the area of the garden?

_____

6. Leticia decided to put a fence around her 6-foot by 8-foot garden. What is the perimeter of the garden?

_____

7. What unit would you use to measure the capacity of a barrel?

_____

8. How many feet are in 120 inches? (Hint: 12 inches = 1 foot)

_____

Name _____ Date _____

Unit 8 Review, page 2

Strategy: Use a Chart

1 pint (pt)	=	2 cups (c)
1 quart (qt)	=	2 pt or 4 c
1 gallon (g)	=	4 qt or 8 pt or 16 c

12 inches (in.)	=	1 foot (ft)
1 yard (yd)	=	3 ft or 36 in.

1 pound (lb)	=	16 ounces (oz)
1 ton (T)	=	2,000 lb

Show What You Know!

Solve each problem using one of the charts.

1. Quila bought 3 yards of material to make her costume for the school play. How many inches of material did she buy?

_____

2. Tamara's fish tank held 5 gallons of water. How many quarts did her fish tank hold?

_____

3. The farm produced 6,000 pounds of potatoes. How many tons of potatoes did the farm produce?

_____

4. Renata bought 64 ounces of ground beef to make hamburgers for a cookout. How many pounds of ground beef did she buy?

_____

5. Danté cut a piece of twine that measured 21 feet long. How many yards of twine did he cut?

_____

Extension ....

Measure the perimeter of your classroom using inches. Change that measurement into feet and yards. Round to the nearest foot and yard.

Problem Solving Strategies 5, SV 0516-2

Name _____ Date _____

FLEX YOUR MATH MUSCLES

1

A farmer left his farm to his wife and four sons. The land was a perfect square. His widow received $\frac{1}{4}$ of the land as shown on the drawing. The other $\frac{3}{4}$ of the farm was divided among his 4 sons with sections of the same size and shape. How was the land divided? Show how the 4 sons shared the land on the drawing.

2

Elia wanted to visit her brother Lorenzo, who lived in River City 100 miles away. She rented a car and drove there. She stopped halfway to River City to pick up her friend, Riane, who rode with her the last 50 miles.

Elia drove back the same evening and dropped Riane off where she had picked her up. Then Elia drove back home and returned the rental car. She paid the bill of $24.00. Elia and Riane agreed to share the cost of the rental car. They each paid their share for the time each was in the car. How much did Elia and Riane each pay?

_____

_____

the farm

wife's land

Problem Solving Strategies 5, SV 0516-2

Name _____ Date _____

DECIMALS AND FRACTIONS

Strategy: Use a Drawing

Decimals, like fractions, show the parts of a whole. The number of places to the right of the decimal point is the number of parts in the whole. You can write fractions and decimals for the same amount. Use this place value chart to read and write decimals.

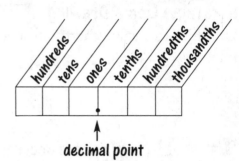

decimal point

STEP 1 ▷ **Read the problem.**
Look at the circle. What part is shaded? Write the fraction and the decimal that show what part of the circle is shaded.

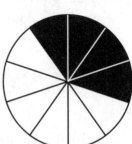

STEP 2 ▷ **Identify the facts.**
The circle has 10 equal parts. 4 parts are shaded.

STEP 3 ▷ **Identify what the problem asks.**
The problem asks what fraction and decimal show the shaded part of the circle.

STEP 4 ▷ **Write a fraction and a decimal. Solve the problem.**
Each part of the circle is $\frac{1}{10}$ or 0.1 of the circle.
4 of the 10 parts of the circle are shaded.
$\frac{4}{10}$ or 0.4 parts are shaded.

Try It! Shade the drawing and write the decimal.

1. Shade the figure to show $\frac{7}{10}$. Write the decimal equivalent.

_____

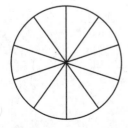

2. Shade the figure to show $\frac{5}{10}$. Write the decimal equivalent.

_____

Name _____ Date _____

DECIMALS AND FRACTIONS, part 2

Strategy: Use a Drawing

Use this place value chart to read and write decimals and fractions.

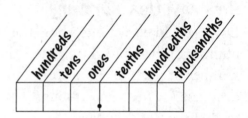

Try It! Write the decimal and fraction.

1. Shade the piles of coins to show the decimal.
   The write the equivalent fraction.

Decimal $0.30   Fraction _____

Decimal $0.60   Fraction _____

2.

Decimal _____

Fraction _____

3.

Decimal _____

Fraction _____

4.

Decimal _____

Fraction _____

Name _____ Date _____

DIZZY DECIMALS

Strategy: Find a Pattern

Some problems are solved by looking for a pattern. Write the rule that makes and completes the pattern.

STEP 1 ▷ **Read the problem.**
What are the next two numbers in this pattern?
1.1   1.3   1.6   2.0   ??   ??

STEP 2 ▷ **Determine the pattern.**
What is the difference between 1.1 and the next number, 1.3?   +0.2
What is the difference between 1.3 and the next number, 1.6?   +0.3
Do the same for all the numbers to find the pattern.

STEP 3 ▷ **Write the pattern.**
Add 0.2, add 0.3, add 0.4, add 0.5, add 0.6, and so on.

STEP 4 ▷ **Solve the problem.**
2.0 + 0.5 = 2.5   2.5 + 0.6 = 3.1

The next two numbers are 2.5 and 3.1.

Try It!   Find and write the pattern. Then solve the problems.

1. What are the next two numbers in this pattern?

$1\frac{2}{10}$ $2\frac{4}{10}$ $3\frac{6}{10}$ $4\frac{8}{10}$ _____   _____

2. What are the next two numbers in this pattern?

9.6   10.8   12   13.2   _____   _____

3. What are the missing numbers in this pattern?

64.0   58.5   53   47.5   _____   _____   31   25.5   _____

4. Jared is saving money to buy a concert ticket. He saved $2.25 the first week, $4.50 the second week, and $6.75 the third week. What is the pattern? How much did he save the fourth week and fifth weeks?

_____

Name _____ Date _____

PLAYFUL PETS

Strategy: Choose an Operation

To solve problems with fractions and decimals, rewrite the problem using all decimals or all fractions. To change a decimal, identify the value of the last place in the decimal. This is the denominator in the fraction.

$$0.7 = \frac{7}{10} \qquad 0.59 = \frac{59}{100} \qquad 0.005 = \frac{5}{1,000}$$

To change a fraction that has a denominator of 10, 100, or 1,000, write the numerator. Then add the decimal point. Use a zero to show that it is less than 1.

$$\frac{3}{10} = 0.3 \qquad \frac{43}{100} = 0.43 \qquad \frac{450}{1,000} = 0.450$$

Try It! Change all decimals or fractions.

1. $\frac{7}{10}$ = _____   **2.** 0.83 = _____   **3.** $\frac{90}{100}$ = _____

4. $\frac{467}{1,000}$ = _____   **5.** 3.52 = _____   **6.** $\frac{500}{1,000}$ = _____

7. $5\frac{3}{10}$ = _____   **8.** 4.07 = _____   **9.** $5\frac{53}{100}$ = _____

10. 0.725 = _____   **11.** $6\frac{35}{100}$ = _____   **12.** 8.008 = _____

Name _____ Date _____

PLAYFUL PETS, part 2

Strategy: Choose an Operation

Sometimes a problem does not tell you the operation. Read the problem carefully and decide what the problem is asking you to do. Change all fractions or all decimals. Then solve the problem.

 Read the problem.

The dog ate 3.6 bowls of food one week and $4\frac{1}{5}$ bowls the next week. How much did he eat in two weeks?

 Identify the facts.

The dog ate 3.6 and $4\frac{1}{5}$ bowls of food.

 Choose an operation.

The problem asks how much the dog ate. You must add to find the total.

 Change to all fractions or all decimals.

$3.6 = 3\frac{6}{10}$ $4\frac{1}{5} = 4\frac{2}{10} = 4.2$

STEP 5 **Add. Solve the problem.**

$$3.6 \ = \quad 3.6 \qquad\qquad 3.6 \ = \quad 3\frac{6}{10}$$
$$4\frac{1}{5} \ = \ +\ 4.2 \qquad\qquad 4\frac{1}{5} \ = \ +\ 4\frac{2}{10}$$
$$\overline{\qquad\qquad} \qquad\qquad\qquad \overline{\qquad\qquad}$$
$$\text{7.8 bowls} \qquad\qquad\qquad 7\frac{8}{10} \text{ bowls}$$

Try It! Choose the operation. Change the fractions or decimals. Solve the problems.

1. The pet shop has 3.25 dozen cat toys and $8\frac{1}{2}$ dozen dog toys. How many dozen toys does the shop have?

_____

2. The owner bought 25.4 lbs of bird seed and $18\frac{3}{10}$ lbs of dog food. How many lbs of animal food did he buy?

_____

Name _____ Date _____

RAMBUNCTIOUS ROVERS

Strategy: Write a Number Sentence

A number sentence shows how numbers are related to each other. Read the problem. Look for clues. Write a number sentence.

STEP 1 **Read the problem.**
Alex sold 2 bags of dog biscuits for a total of 35 biscuits. He put 23.5 biscuits in one bag. How many biscuits were in the other bag?

STEP 2 **List the clues.**
Clue 1: He sold 2 bags.
Clue 2: He put 23.5 biscuits in one bag.
Clue 3: He sold 35 biscuits in all.

STEP 3 **Write a number sentence.**
? + 23.5 = 35 biscuits

STEP 4 **Subtract. Solve the problem.**
35 − 23.5 = ?

11.5 biscuits in the other bag

Try It! Look for clues. Change to all fractions or all decimals. Write a number sentence. Solve the problems.

1. Paul's two dogs buried $4\frac{1}{2}$ bones. One dog buried 2.25 bones. How many bones did the other dog bury?

   _____

2. Carol's dogs dug a hole 3.75 feet deep. The neighbor's dogs came over and dug a hole $4\frac{1}{4}$ feet deep. How many feet deeper was the hole dug by the neighbor's dogs?

   _____

3. Steve measured the doghouse. It was 17.75 square feet in area. The yard was $82\frac{1}{4}$ square feet bigger than the doghouse. What is the area of the yard?

   _____

4. Thomasin knitted a coat and hat for her dog. She used a total of 2.9 skeins of yarn. She used $\frac{6}{10}$ skeins for the hat. How much yarn did she use for the coat?

   _____

Problem Solving Strategies 5, SV 0516-2

Name _____ Date _____

FEATHER YOUR NEST

Strategy: Use Estimation

You can solve some problems by estimating. Find the estimate by rounding some or all the numbers to the same place. When a number is halfway to the nearest place, round up. You can use a number line to round decimals.

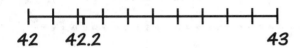

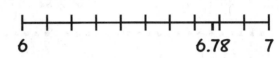

42.2 is closer to 42 than to 43.
42.2 rounds down to 42.

6.78 is closer to 7 than to 6.
6.78 rounds up to 7.

STEP 1 **Read the problem.**
Mario was birdwatching. He walked 3.8 miles and found chickadee feathers. He walked another 2.3 miles and found cardinal feathers. About how far did he walk?

STEP 2 **Identify the facts.**
He walked 3.8 miles and 2.3 miles.

STEP 3 **Estimate by rounding the numbers to the same place.**
3.8 can be rounded to 4.0 because the numeral after the decimal point is more than halfway to the nearest place. 2.3 can be rounded down to 2 because 2.3 is less than halfway to 3.0.

STEP 4 **Estimate by adding the rounded numbers. Solve the problem.**
4 + 2 = 6   Mario walked about 6 miles.

Try It! Estimate by rounding. Solve the problems.

1. Mario found some seashells at a depth of 4.6 feet. He found more seashells at 2.3 feet. About how much deeper were the first seashells?

_____

2. The nests in the tree were at various distances from the ground. The first was at 1.4 meters. The second was 1.3 meters beyond the first. The third was 1.6 meters beyond the second. About how far was the third nest from the ground?

_____

Problem Solving Strategies 5, SV 0516-2

Name _____ Date _____

Unit 9 Review

Strategies

- Use a Drawing
- Use a Chart
- Find a Pattern
- Choose an Operation
- Write a Number Sentence
- Use Estimation

Show What You Know!

Solve each problem. Identify the strategy you used.

---

1. Use the place value chart to write the decimal equivalent of $327\frac{35}{100}$.

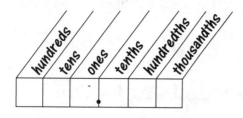

_____

2. Write the decimal and the fraction.

_____

3. Shade the figure to show $\frac{4}{10}$. Write the decimal equivalent.

_____

4. Peter bought 4.2 pounds of wheat flour and $3\frac{6}{10}$ pounds of corn flour. How many pounds of flour did Peter buy?

_____

5. Write $\frac{3}{10}$ as a decimal.

_____

6. Write the decimal and the fraction.

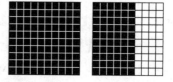

_____

7. A messenger drives 2.5 miles to her first stop, 4 miles to her second stop, and 5.5 miles to her third stop. If this pattern continues, how far will she drive to her fourth and fifth stops?

_____

Name _____ Date _____

Unit 9 Review, page 2

Show What You Know!

Solve each problem. Identify the strategy you used.

1. What are the next two numbers in this pattern?

   5.5   7.6   9.7   11.8   ____   ____

2. Clarisa bought 5.2 pounds of beef and $3\frac{7}{10}$ pounds of chicken. How many pounds of meat did Clarisa buy?

   _____

3. Jerrell walked 1.7 miles on Monday, 2.4 miles on Tuesday, and 1.9 miles on Wednesday. About how many miles did he walk altogether?

   _____

4. What are the next two numbers in this pattern?

   21.5   17.8   14.1   10.4   ____   ____

5. Felicity cut 7.2 feet of blue ribbon. She used 1.9 feet to decorate the first package and 3.3 feet to decorate the second package. About how much ribbon did Felicity have left to use for other packages?

   _____

6. Use the place value chart to write the decimal equivalent of $46\frac{21}{1,000}$.

   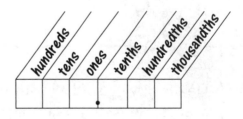

   _____

Extension

On a piece of paper, trace the outline of your foot. Use a ruler to measure the length of your foot from the heel to the tip of your big toe. Round the measurement to the nearest $\frac{1}{4}$ inch. Then write the decimal equivalent of the fraction.

FLEX YOUR MATH MUSCLES

1

Flex has a problem. He knows that if he adds $10 + $10, the sum is $20. What is the total if he multiplies $10 × $10?

_____

_____

2

Flex's aunt had 9 diamonds all the same size. She took them to a jeweler who checked them out. He gave her some bad news. One of the diamonds was a fake! The jeweler put them on his scale. In three weighings, he was able to find the phony diamond. It was lighter than the others. How did he do this?

_____

_____

_____

3

Flex is playing softball with his friends. He is only a fair hitter with a batting average of .200. What does this mean? How many hits does she get in 10 times at bat?

_____

_____

Do you play baseball? Can you figure your batting average?

Name _____ Date _____

HOORAY FOR METRICS!

Strategy: Use Estimation

The meter is the basic metric unit of length. A baseball bat is about 1 meter long. A kilometer (km) is 1,000 meters. *Kilo* means 1,000. The kilometer is used to measure long distances or lengths. A centimeter is $\frac{1}{100}$ of a meter, just as a cent is $\frac{1}{100}$ of a dollar. The centimeter is used to measure short distances or lengths.

centimeter (cm)	meter (m)	kilometer (km)
0.01 m	0.001 km	1,000 m
	100 cm	

STEP 1 ▷ **Define the length or distance as short, medium, or long.**

distance between 2 cities   long

STEP 2 ▷ **Identify the appropriate unit.**

Long distances are measured in kilometers.

STEP 3 ▷ **Estimate the length. Solve the problem.**

distance between 2 cities   ___km___

Try It!   Estimate the length and identify the appropriate unit. Use cm, m, or km.

1. the length of your classroom   _____

2. the length of a piece of chalk   _____

3. the length of your shoe   _____

4. the width of your favorite book   _____

5. the length of a football field   _____

6. the length of a marathon race path   _____

7. the height of a tree   _____

8. the length of a river   _____

HOORAY FOR METRICS! part 2

Strategy: Choose an Operation

A centimeter (cm) is one-hundredth of a meter. *Centi* means 0.01. The centimeter is used to measure small lengths such as a pencil. A millimeter (mm) is one thousandth of a meter. *Milli* means 0.001. The millimeter is used to measure very small lengths such as the length of a housefly.

---

1 meter (m) = 100 centimeters (cm)	1 meter (m) = 1,000 millimeters (mm)
1 cm = 0.01 meters	1 mm = 0.001 meters
1 cm = 10 mm	

To change from cm to mm, multiply by 10. To change from mm to cm, divide by 10.

STEP 1 **Read the problem.**
A paper clip is 3 cm long. How many mm long is it?

STEP 2 **Choose the operation.**
To change from cm to mm, multiply by 10.

STEP 3 **Multiply. Solve the problem.**
3 cm × 10 = 30 cm

Try It! Use the chart and choose an operation to solve the problems.

1. The width of a sheet of paper is about 200 mm.
How many cm wide is it? _____

2. A pencil is about 15 cm long.
How many mm long is it? _____

3. A leaf on a plant is about 35 mm long.
How many cm long is it? _____

4. A fingernail is about 12 mm long.
How many cm long is it? _____

5. An eraser is about 5.5 cm long.
How many mm long is it? _____

Name _____ Date _____

METRIC WEIGHT

Strategy: Use Estimation

The gram (g) is the basic metric unit of weight. The gram is used to measure the weight of a very light object, for example, a paper clip.

A kilogram (kg) is 1,000 grams. It is used to measure the weight of heavier objects. Use kg for the weight of a dictionary. Remember, *kilo* means 1,000.

1 kilogram (kg) = 1,000 grams (g)	1 gram (g) = 0.001 kilogram (kg)

Try It! How would you measure the weight of these items? Use g or kg.

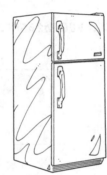

1. a telephone book _____

2. a nickel _____

3. a refrigerator _____

4. you _____

5. a pencil _____

Try It! Circle the best measurement for the weight of these items.

6. a dog   9 g   9 kg

7. a bicycle   18 g   18 kg

8. a loaf of bread   500 g   500 kg

9. a cup   30 g   30 kg

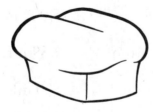

10. a spoon   8 g   8 kg

Problem Solving Strategies 5, SV 0516-2

METRIC MEASURES IN A GLASS

Strategy: Use Estimation

The liter (L) is the basic metric unit of capacity. A liter of liquid will fill a box 10 centimeters on each side.

A milliliter (mL) is 0.001 liter. It is used to measure very small amounts of liquid. A milliliter of liquid will fill a box 1 centimeter on each side.

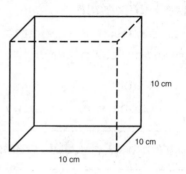

| 1 liter (L) = 1,000 milliliter (mL) | 1 milliliter (mL) = 0.001 liter (L) |

Try It! How would you measure the capacity of these items? Use mL or L.

1. a tank truck _____

2. a gas tank _____

3. a teapot _____

4. a teacup _____

5. a thimble _____

Try It! Circle the best measurement for the capacity of these items.

6. a swimming pool   5,000 mL   5,000 L

7. an orange juice carton   1.89 mL   1.89 L

8. a teapot   700 mL   700 L

9. a soup bowl   180 mL   180 L

10. a contact lens case   40 mL   40 L

Name _____ Date _____

ARE WE RELATED?

Strategy: Use a Chart

You have studied some of the metric units. The basic units are meter (m), liter (L), and gram (g). They are used with prefixes such as *kilo-* and *centi-* to form larger and smaller units. For example, *kilogram* means *kilo-* plus *gram* (kg). Kg means 1,000 grams (g). Kg is larger than g. *Centimeter* means *centi-* plus *meter* (cm). Cm means 0.01 m. Cm is smaller than m. The chart shows the smallest unit of measure at the bottom, and the largest unit at the top.

Prefix	Symbol	Meaning
kilo-	k	1,000
hecto-	h	100
deka-	da	10
base unit	m, L, g	1
deci-	d	0.1
centi-	c	0.01
milli-	m	0.001

STEP 1 **Read the problem.**
Which is larger, 10 decimeters (dm) or 10 centimeters (cm)?

STEP 2 **Identify what the problem asks.**
The problem asks to compare 10 decimeters and 10 centimeters.

STEP 3 **Use the metric chart.**
Find the unit in the chart. Move to the new unit.
1 dm = 0.1 m
1 cm = 0.01 m

STEP 4 **Solve the problem.**
10 dm > 10 cm

Try It! Use the metric chart. Solve the problems.

1. Which is greater, 50 cm or 50 mm?

_____

2. What is smaller, 5 kg or 5 dg?

_____

3. Which is larger, 10 mL or 10 L?

_____

4. What is smaller, 100 dm or 100 cm?

_____

CHANGING UNITS

Strategy: Choose an Operation

The metric system is based on 10s. To change from one metric unit to another, multiply or divide. Look at the chart. To move to a smaller unit, multiply. To move to a larger unit, divide.

Prefix	Symbol	Meaning
kilo-	k	1,000
hecto-	h	100
deka-	da	10
base unit	m, L, g	1
deci-	d	0.1
centi-	c	0.01
milli-	m	0.001

2 km = (2 × 1,000) m   600 cm = (600 ÷ 100) m
2 km = 2,000 m   600 cm = 6 m

STEP 1 ▷ **Read the problem.**
How many meters is 2 km?

STEP 2 ▷ **Identify what the problem asks. Choose an operation.**
The problem asks to change 2 km to meters. To find the metric equivalent, look at the chart. Meter is a smaller unit than kilometer. You should multiply.

STEP 3 ▷ **Write the equivalent from the chart.**
km = 1,000 meters

STEP 4 ▷ **Multiply. Solve the problem.**
2 km = (2 × 1,000) m
2 km = 2,000 m

Try It! Use the metric chart. Choose an operation. Solve the problems.

1. Celia has 2 kilograms (kg) of pasta. How many grams (g) does she have?

_____

2. Deven has a Spanish book that weighs 0.65 kg. Carmen has a French book that weighs 600 grams. Who has the lighter book?

_____

3. Jenny ran in a 10 km race. How many meters did she run?

_____

4. If Derrick adds 230 mL of milk to the 0.4 L of milk in a pitcher, how much milk will be in the pitcher?

_____

Name _____   Date _____

Unit 10 Review

Show What You Know!

Solve each problem. Identify the strategy you used.

1. Would you use centimeters, meters, or kilometers to measure the length of your shirt sleeve? Estimate the length of your shirt sleeve.

_____

2. How many meters is 5 kilometers?

_____

3. How many centimeters is 9 meters?

_____

4. Would you use liters or milliliters to measure the capacity of a fishing pond?

_____

5. Would you use centimeters, meters, or kilometers to measure the length of a river?

_____

6. How many millimeters is 50 centimeters?

_____

7. Would you use liters or milliliters to measure the capacity of a rain gauge?

_____

8. How many grams is 2 kilograms?

_____

Unit 10 Review, page 2

Metric Chart

Prefix	Symbol	Meaning
kilo-	k	1,000
hecto-	h	100
deka-	da	10
base unit	m, L, g	1
deci-	d	0.1
centi-	c	0.01
milli-	m	0.001

> **Strategy**
> • Use a Chart

Show What You Know!

Use the chart to solve each problem.

1. Which is greater, 50 decimeters or 50 dekameters?

_____

2. Paula ran a 3 km race. How many meters did she run?

_____

3. Kennedy saw that his snack had 2 grams of fat. How many milligrams of fat were in his snack?

_____

4. Which is greater, 25 liters or 25 milliliters?

_____

5. Shaniqua measured the length of her desk. It was about 1 meter long. About how many centimeters long was her desk?

_____

Extension

Measure the length of this page with a centimeter ruler. Round to the nearest centimeter. What is the length of this page in millimeters? What is the length of this page in meters?

Name _____ Date _____

FLEX YOUR MATH MUSCLES

1

Flex and his friend Maria collect arrowheads.
They have 24 arrowheads.

They packed the arrowheads in a box in 6 equal
rows. Half were in good condition. Six were
broken. Six had holes in them.

They took the box to a jeweler. He wanted 18
of the 24 heads in the box. He wanted the best
ones. He offered $100 apiece for them. He
offered $50 apiece for the ones he did not want.

Flex and Maria decided to take the arrowheads
to another jeweler. He offered them $1,500 for
all the arrowheads.

Should they return to the first jeweler, or should
they sell the arrowheads to the second jeweler?

_____

Why? _____

_____

Problem Solving Strategies 5, SV 0516-2

Name _____ Date _____

IT'S YOUR CHOICE

Strategy: Choose a Strategy

You have worked with several different strategies for problem solving. Choose a strategy.

Choose an Operation	Make a Drawing	Use Guess and Check	Identify Substeps
Use a Chart	Use Logic	Use Estimation	Work Backward

Try It! Choose a strategy from the list to solve each problem.

1. Jim lives 450 yards east of Lincoln School. Tim lives 542 yards west of the school. How far apart from each other do Jim and Tim live?

Strategy _____

Answer _____

2. Yoshi has 52 stamps and 85 envelopes. She bought 20 stamps and 50 envelopes this morning. How many of each did she have before today?

Strategy _____

Answer _____

3. You have $51 to spend on shirts. They cost $11.25 each. Can you buy 5 shirts?

Strategy _____

Answer _____

4. Mary, Robert, and Cindy met at the pool. One walked, one rode a bike, and one skated. Mary does not have skates. The one who walked had to tie his shoes. Cindy does not have a bike. How did each of them get to the pool?

Strategy _____

Answer _____

_____

_____

5. The school cook ordered 350 loaves of bread. If each loaf has 12 slices, how many slices of bread are there?

Strategy _____

Answer _____

6. You have 4 coins totaling $0.37. What are they?

Strategy _____

Answer _____

_____

Choose a Strategy
Problem Solving Strategies 5, SV 0516-2

Answer Key

NOTE: Students may use different strategies to solve problems on the unit reviews. Strategies listed are most likely. Ask students to explain their strategies to ensure understanding.

Page 6
1. line
2. $10.50
3. 23 comic books
4. 10 cards
5. Jorge: 16; Julia: 15
6. 72 prizes

Page 7
7. 500 miles
8. 4/12
9. 2-1/6 pies
10. 1st: Yvonne; 2nd: Elena; 3rd: Jerry
11. 25 square feet

Page 8
12. gallon
13. 5 tons
14. 42, 36.5, 20
15. 2.25 bones or 2-1/4 bones
16. Use estimation. no

Page 9
1. fiction
2. biography
3. fiction
4. taller bar
5. 250 books
6. 1,300 books

Page 10
1. white
2. oat
3. white
4. wheat
5. 30 loaves
6. 220 loaves

Page 11
1. Saturday
2. Saturday
3. 10 more pizzas
4. sausage, taller bars

Page 12
1. 10 percent
2. Oct. and Mar.
3. 20 percent
4. Nov., Feb., Apr.
5. Dec.
6. Feb.–May

Page 13
1. 2006
2. Oct. and Nov. 2006
3. Sept., Feb., and Apr.
4. Dec. 2005 and Feb. 2006
5. Mar.
6. Feb.

Page 14
1. taxes
2. insurance and auto or taxes and housing
3. $2,000
4. $550

Page 15
Answers may vary.
1. bar
2. line
3. line
4. pie
5. line
6. bar
7. pie
8. bar

Page 16
1. line
2. pie
3. bar
4. pie
5. line
6. bar

Page 17
1. almonds
2. walnuts
3. 500 pounds
4. 2 pounds
5. 4 months old
6. 5 pounds

Page 18
1, 17
1. 2
2. 3
3. 3
4. 1
5. 1
6. prime numbers
7. 23, 29

Page 20
1. canary: Ann; hamster: Beth
2. 1st: Yvonne; 2nd: Elena; 3rd: Jerry
3. Donna: swim; Linda: softball; Sandi: basketball; Nancy: track

Page 21
4. doctor's office: 1st floor; lawyer's office: 2nd floor; accountant's office: 3rd floor

Page 22
1. green
2. blue
3. white

Page 23
1. Ms. Bernal
2. Mr. Robinson
3. Mr. Peterson
4. Ms. Sorenson

Page 24
1. hamburgers
2. egg rolls
3. spaghetti
4. tacos

Page 25
1. astronomy
2. geography
3. chemistry
4. oceanography

Page 26
1.

First	Anna
Second	Tyrone
Third	Katy
Fourth	Ira
Fifth	Pete

Tyrone won 2nd place.

2.

5 (Heaviest)	Box C
4	Box E
3	Box D
2	Box B
1 (Lightest)	Box A

Box C was the heaviest.

Page 27
1.

10:00 P.M.	Mr. and Mrs. Sanders
9:00 P.M.	Bird
8:00 P.M.	Man with Flat Tire
7:00 P.M.	Mr. Sanders
6:00 P.M.	Delivery Boy

The man with the flat tire is the most likely suspect.
2. Shameka plays the drums. Wendy plays the flute. Caleb plays the violin. Artuto plays the tuba.

Page 28
1. 31 students
2. 7 students

Page 29
1. ~~She has $25.~~ She gives the clerk a $20 bill. He gives her $9.50 change. $10.50
2. ~~Your brother is selling cookie dough containers for $4 each.~~ He has sold 25 containers. He needs to sell a total of 86 to win a prize. 61 containers.
3. Your father buys 8.5 gallons of gas. ~~He also buys 1 quart of oil for $1.75~~ Gas costs $1.40 per gallon. $11.90
4. ~~Your sister buys dog food once a month.~~ She feeds the dog 112 ounces of dog food each week. 16 ounces a day.

Page 30
1. ~~The sales tax is $0.96.~~ $17.15
2. ~~and 6 dogs in the evening.~~ $2.00
3. ~~He also bought 3 books for $3 each.~~ $10
4. ~~She saves $100 from her pay.~~ $210
5. ~~She jogs between 2 and 3 miles every school day.~~ 5 hours
6. ~~She practices for 60 minutes every Saturday and Sunday.~~ 150 minutes

Page 31
Answers will vary.
1. 2,700 customers
2. 132,000 fans
3. $30,000
4. 600 copies
5. 300 photos
6. $40

Page 32
Answers will vary.
1. 20 bushes
2. 500 mph
3. 90 pounds
4. 500 miles
5. 4,000,000 people
6. 10 gallons

Page 33
1. 171 plants
2. 84 geraniums
3. 29 marigold plants
4. 21 petunia plants

Page 34
1. 59 cards
2. 91 cards
3. 23 comic books
4. 40 seashells

Page 35
1. $51.30
2. $1.11
3. 52 disks
4. $42.33

Page 36
1. $7.43; Identify Extra Information
2. 8 planes; Work Backward
3. About 50 miles; Use Estimation
4. 22 books; Identify Substeps
5. About 80 points; Use Estimation

Page 37
1. 52 inches; Add; Choose an Operation
2. 17 bracelets; Work Backward
3. 64 years old; Identify Extra Information
4. 16 tickets; Identify Substeps

Page 38
Answers will vary.

Page 39
1. 72 prizes
2. 48 candies
3. 150 minutes
4. 12 people
5. 33 times
6. 56 balloons

Page 40
1. 10 cards
2. Phyllis gets 1 more card.

Page 41
1. Jorge: 16; Julia: 15
2. $21
3. pages 14 and 15
4. hammer: $27; saw: $21

Page 42
1. 1,800 pages
2. $2.00
3. 4 problems
4. 8 miles

Page 43
1. Extra fact: Alpha and Beta galaxies are 3,657 light-years apart.
2. Extra fact: It carries a crew of 1,500 space cadets, regulars, and officers.
   Missing fact: distance and rate of speed.

Page 44
1. Extra fact: Last year, there were 500 students enrolled in the Academy.
2. Missing fact: how much 1 barrel is worth.
3. Missing fact: how many tons of ore 1 space freighter can carry.
4. Missing fact: how many Merkians traveled to other planets during the last 15 years.

Page 45
1. 130 riders
2. $1,200
3. 48,000 people
4. 2,400 bikes

Page 46
1. Lee's plant = 8 inches; Clay's plant = 4 inches; Guess and Check, Choose an Operation
2. 35 letters; Identify Substeps, Choose an Operation
3. About 160; Use Estimation
4. 5 years; Work Backward

Page 47
1. This problem cannot be solved because you do not know how many pencils are in each package.; Identify Extra or Missing Information
2. 40 pounds; Choose an Operation
3. $2.00; Identify Substeps, Choose an Operation
4. 18 pages; Identify Extra or Missing Information, Choose an Operation
5. Monday = 2 miles; Tuesday = 4 miles; Guess and Check, Choose an Operation

Page 48
1. $5,887.20
2. He can tell if he has 1/2 pound (8 ounces) of gold or 1 pound (16 ounces) of gold.
3. He can tell if he has 1/4 pound (4 ounces), 1/2 pound (8 ounces), 3/4 pound (12 ounces), or 1 pound (16 ounces) of gold.
4. He can break up the remaining 15 ounces into 1-ounce pieces and use them for his weights to measure up to 15 ounces of gold in 1-ounce increments.
5. $4,415.40

Page 49
1. 36 potatoes
2. Wells bars are 6¢ less expensive.
3. 162 baskets
4. 96¢ for a half dozen

Page 50
1. 7 mail routes
2. 10 hours

Page 51
1. 64 pages
2. 99 pages

Page 52
1. Ann: 22 prizes; Ben: 44 prizes; Cara: 30 prizes
2. $5.00
3. 76 tickets
4. $10.00

Page 53
Answers may vary.
1. 500 miles
2. 100 planes
3. 500 miles
4. 20 groups

Page 54
1. ham: 5 pieces; turkey: 12 pieces; meatballs: 4

Page 55
1. ham: 10 pieces; turkey: 6 pieces; meatballs: 3
2. ham: $2.50; turkey: $2.25; meatball: $2.65

Page 56
1. 4 roses; Choose an Operation
2. Suki is 16, Min is 8, and Chen is 6.; Work Backward
3. 5 miles; Choose an Operation
4. $1.00 per leash; 25 cents per treat; 50 cents per toy; Identify Substeps, Choose an Operation
5. 4 bookcases; 8 shelves per bookcase; Guess and Check

Page 57
1. 35 students; Guess and Check
2. 600 miles; Use Estimation
3. Each school got 25 shirts.; Make a Table.

Problem Solving Strategies 5, SV 0516-2

Page 58

1. Flex can cross the desert with the help of only 2 friends. At the end of the first day, each person has 3 days' worth of supplies left. 1 person returns to the starting point carrying 1 day's worth of supplies and leaving the rest for Flex and the 1 friend who is staying with him. They each then have 4 days' worth of supplies, 3 that they started with and 1 from the friend who went back. At the end of the second day, Flex and his friend each have 3 days' worth of supplies left. The second friend returns to the starting point with 2 days' worth of supplies to get there, leaving Flex with 1 additional day's worth of supplies. This gives Flex 4 days' worth of supplies, which is enough to get him to his destination.

2. Look at the picture of the books on the shelf. Page 1 of Volume 1 and the last page of Volume 2 are only separated by the covers. The bookworm had eaten through 1/4 inch of the books before he was discovered and terminated!

3. 1,966 pennies equal $19.66, which is almost $20.

Page 59

1. 1/6
2. 2/3
3. 4/7
4. 4/12 or 1/3

Page 60

1. 4/8
2. 4/8
3. 1/2 Answers will vary.

Page 61

1. 3/6 or 1/2
2. 6/8 or 3/4

Page 62

1. 1/2
2. 1/4

Page 63

1. 11/12

Page 64

1. 2/3 of an hour; 40 minutes
2. 7/10 of her homework; 3/10 more

Page 65

1. 11/4; 2-3/4
2. 1-1/2; 1-1/4; 1-2/3

Page 66

1. 5/10 = 1/2; Use a Drawing
2. 7/12; Use a Drawing
3. 1/6; Choose an Operation, Write a Number Sentence
4. 12/15 = 4/5; Make a Drawing, Write a Number Sentence, Choose an Operation
5. 5/8; Choose an Operation

Page 67

1. 2/3; Write a Number Sentence
2. 3/6 (or 1/2); Choose an Operation
3. 7/20; Make a Drawing, Write a Number Sentence, Choose an Operation
4. 8/12 (or 2/3); Use a Drawing

Page 68

1. 5/12
2. 7/10
3. 2/10 or 1/5
4. 3/15 or 1/5
5. 4/10 or 2/5 miles

Page 69

1. 2/3   2. 1/6

Page 70

1. 5/12 of the pie
2. 1/12 more

Page 71

1. 2-1/6 pies
2. 10 pies

Page 72

1. 2-13/20 pies
2. 1-1/6 pies

Page 73

1. 4-3/8 bags
2. 2-1/4 dozen

Page 74

1. Extra fact: Grandmother Hubbard baked for the twins who are 11 years old. 5-7/8 cakes

2. Extra fact: Her neighbor blew up 5 balloons. 1-1/3 dozen

Page 75

1. 5/12 of the water
2. 1/6 of her flowers
3. 2-3/4 dozen left
4. 2-2/3 tarts left
5. 2-1/15 bags of coins left
6. 9-3/4 hours in all
7. 2-5/12 feet higher
8. 14-5/6 miles in all

Page 76

1. 7/12; Find Equivalent Fractions, Choose an Operation
2. 7 pizzas; Choose an Operation, Find Equivalent Fractions
3. 1/12; Identify Extra or Missing Information, Find Equivalent Fractions, Choose an Operation
4. 5/6 hour; Find Equivalent Fractions
5. 3/8 foot; Find Equivalent Fractions, Choose an Operation

Page 77

1. 3/6 = 1/2; Find Equivalent Fractions, Choose an Operation
2. 5/8 pound; Find Equivalent Fractions
3. 3-3/4 bags; Change Whole Numbers to Fractions
4. 2-1/2 dozen; Identify Extra or Missing Information, Find Equivalent Fractions, Choose an Operation
5. I do not know what fraction Roger traded with Sue.; Identify Extra or Missing Information

Page 78

1. Flex fills the 5-gallon can and pours it into the 8-gallon can. He fills the 5-gallon can again and pours as much as he can into the 8-gallon can. The 8-gallon can can take 3 more gallons from the 5-gallon can. This leaves 2 gallons in the 5-gallon can.

2. A $10 gold coin contains $10 worth of gold and a $20 gold coin contains $20 worth of gold. If gold is worth about $400 an ounce, 2 pounds of gold would be worth $12,800 and 4 pounds would be worth $25,600!

3. There are 23 rungs on the ladder.

Page 79

1. 180 square feet
2. 25 square feet
3. 18 square feet

Page 80

Answers will vary.
1. pint
2. cup
3. gallon
4. gallon
5. cup
6. quart
7. gallon
8. pint

Page 81

1. 2
2. 4
3. 3
4. 16
5. 32
6. 5

Page 82

1. 24 feet
2. 180 inches
3. 100 yards
4. 20 yards

Page 84

1. 10 pounds
2. 4 pounds
3. 6,000 pounds
4. 7 tons
5. 160 ounces
6. 2 pounds
7. 5 tons
8. 128 ounces

Page 85

1. 160 ft
2. 676 ft
3. 800 yd
4. 1,312 ft

Page 86

1. 24 pints; Choose an Operation
2. 96 square feet; Use a Formula
3. 40 feet; Use a Formula

Page 86, continued
4. gallons; Use Estimation
5. 48 square feet; Use a Formula
6. 28 feet; Use a Formula
7. gallons; Use Estimation
8. 10 feet; Choose an Operation

Page 87
1. 108 in.
2. 20 qt
3. 3 T
4. 4 lb
5. 7 yd

Page 88
1. Answers will vary. Sample:

2. Elia rode twice as long as Riane. Therefore, Elia paid twice as much as Riane. Since the total was $24, Riane paid $8 and Elia paid $16.

Page 89
1. 0.7
2. 0.5

Page 90
1. 3/10; 6/10
2. 2.3; 2-3/10
3. 1.75; 1-75/100 or 1-3/4
4. 3.1; 3-1/10

Page 91
1. 6, 7-2/10
2. 14.4, 15.6
3. 42, 36.5, 20
4. $9.00, $11.25

Page 92
1. 0.7   7. 5.3
2. 83/100   8. 4-7/100
3. 0.90   9. 5.53
4. 0.467   10. 725/1,000
5. 3-52/100   11. 6.35
6. 0.500   12. 8-8/1,000

Page 93
1. 11.75 or 11-75/100 or 11-3/4 dozen
2. 43.7 or 43-7/10 pounds

Page 94
1. 2.25 or 2-1/4 bones
2. 0.5 or 1/2 foot
3. 100 square feet
4. 2.3 or 2-3/10 skeins

Page 95
Answers will vary.
1. 3 feet
2. 4 meters

Page 96
1. 327.35; Use a Chart
2. 2.30; 2-30/100; Use a Drawing
3.

0.4; Use a Drawing
4. 7.8 lb; Choose an Operation, Write a Number Sentence
5. 0.3; Choose an Operation
6. 1.60; 1-60/100 Use a Drawing
7. 7 miles, 8.5 miles; Find a Pattern

Page 97
1. 13.9, 16; Find a Pattern
2. 8.9 lb; Choose an Operation, Write a Number Sentence
3. About 6 miles; Use Estimation, Write a Number Sentence, Choose an Operation
4. 6.7, 3; Find a Pattern
5. About 2 feet; Use Estimation, Write a Number Sentence, Choose an Operation
6. 46.021; Use a Chart

Page 98
1. You can't multiply or divide dollars by dollars.
2. The jeweler divides the 9 diamonds in 3 groups of 3 diamonds each. He puts 1 group of diamonds on each pan of his balance scale. If they balance, he knows that the fake diamond is in the third group. He puts the first 2 groups aside and takes 2 of the 3 diamonds from the third group and puts 1 on each pan of the scale. If they balance, he knows that the third diamond is the fake. If they don't balance, then the lighter one is the fake. He can determine which one is the fake one in a maximum of 3 weighings.
3. In baseball, a batting average of .200 means the hitter gets 2 hits in 10 times at bat.

Page 99
Answers may vary.
1. m   5. m
2. cm   6. km
3. cm   7. m
4. cm   8. km

Page 100
1. 20 cm
2. 150 mm
3. 3.5 cm
4. 1.2 cm
5. 55 mm

Page 101
Answers may vary.
1. kg
2. g
3. kg
4. kg
5. g
6. 9 kg
7. 18 kg
8. 500 g
9. 30 g
10. 8 g

Page 102
Answers may vary.
1. L
2. L
3. L
4. mL
5. mL
6. 5,000 L
7. 1.89 L
8. 700 mL
9. 180 mL
10. 40 mL

Page 103
1. 50 cm
2. 5 dg
3. 10 L
4. 100 cm

Page 104
1. 2,000 g
2. Carmen
3. 10,000 m
4. 630 mL or 0.63 L

Page 105
1. cm; Answers will vary.; Use Estimation
2. 5,000 m; Choose an Operation
3. 900 cm; Choose an Operation
4. L; Use Estimation
5. km; Use Estimation
6. 500 mm; Choose an Operation
7. mL; Use Estimation
8. 2,000 g; Choose an Operation

Page 106
1. 50 dam
2. 3,000 m
3. 2,000 mg
4. 25 L
5. 100 cm

Page 107
1. They should return to the first jeweler because he offered them more money.

Page 108
Strategies may vary.
1. Choose an Operation. 992 yards
2. Work Backward. 32 stamps; 35 envelopes
3. Use Estimation. no
4. Use Logic. Mary rode a bike. Robert walked. Cindy skated.
5. Choose an Operation. 4,200 slices
6. Use Guess and Check. 1 quarter, 1 dime, 2 pennies

Problem Solving Strategies 5, SV 0516-2